I WAS A BRITISH WAR BRIDE WORLD WAR II

Kathleen Price

Published by FWB Publications, Columbus, Ohio
Published in the United States of America
ISBN: 9798556536333 |Autobiography

Table Of Contents

KATHLEEN PRICE

AGE 94

ACKNOWLEDGMENTS

Thank You To My Friend, Agnes; Who Helped Organize My Manuscript.
Thank You To My Special Friend, Jane; For Standing By Me For Many
Years.
A Special Thank You To My Four Children; Paul, Bill, Kathy, And
Sheila, And Their Families For Their Unconditional Love And Support

CHAPTER
1

1926

My story begins on September 6, 1926. My given name was Kathleen Ella Hagger. Parents were Arthur Hagger and Violet Ward Hagger. I was born on my maternal grandfather's farm at Swanland Dale Swanland, E. Yorkshire, England. A strange story because I really don't know who I am. By the time I became aware that Arthur Hagger was not my real father, my mother had passed away. The only person who could have told me who my father was had also passed away about 3 months previous to my inquiry. The only other information I had after my discovery was from my aunts, Dora and Dolly, my mother's two sisters.

This is the way it was told to me. At the age of nineteen, my mother became pregnant with me, my father was a British soldier stationed at Fulford near York. He was from a very prominent family; in those days there was a marked difference in the classes. My mother was the daughter of a well-known Yorkshire Farmer, a commoner who was beneath the soldier's station in life. According to information I received, the soldier was transferred to some place unknown to my mother, and she never saw him again. He had a sister in London who, apparently offered to adopt me. Her name was Kathleen and I assume I was named after her. I have struggled with all this information, and often wonder who I am. My only consolation is that God knows. This is the only part of my story that I cannot confirm. The remainder is the true story of my life as I have lived it. Therefore, I leave it in God's Hands and His care.

THE EARLY YEARS

One of my first memories was living in a bungalow at Holme on Spalding Moore, E. Yorkshire. It was located at the bottom of Holme Church Hill. The Grand Old Church of England could be seen for miles in all directions. I have only fleeting memories of the following incident mostly from my mother's information. I was 2 years old; it was cold outside and mother had let the fire burn low in order to clean the fireplace; I was seated in my highchair in front of the fire while she was doing the rest of the cleaning. I wanted down from my chair and before she could reach me I raised the tray of the chair and stepped forward. The chair tipped over and I fell with my face in the fire grate among the red-hot cinders. I was immediately rushed to the Village Doctor's Surgery (office) a distance of about a half a mile.

There was a new experiment at the time; a substance was sprayed on my face that set to a hard consistency and remained on for six weeks. I recall one day when walking with mother to the doctor's surgery (office) for a checkup, we stopped on the way to see Aunty Dora who lived close by. After the period of time allotted, the substance was peeled off, and my skin was practically free of scars but never smooth. As the years have passed it is not noticeable. I do remember what that cottage looked like on the inside and where the fireplace was located. The cottage is still there but has been remodeled.

I was almost four when we moved to Lincoln Flats, a duplicate house by the railroad tracks (known as a double in America) located on Selby Rd. Most of my early memories were from the time when we lived there. I loved everything about the house and the large garden and orchard. Several yards from the house next door were two gates where the main road crossed the railroad tracks. These gates had to remain closed across the railroad tracks, and were to be opened before a train would approach. When opened, the gates would cross the main road over the railroad tracks. Inside the house was a signal box with an alarm that sounded when a train was scheduled to leave the station at the village of Foggathorpe. This alarm meant 'OPEN THE GATES IMMEDIATELY.' Believe me it took a strong man to be able operate those gates.

NOVEMBER 1930

MY BABY BROTHER ARRIVED

He was born on November 13 1930 at the home of Granny Hagger in Hull E.Yorkshire. I always enjoyed visiting there because that was where my cousin Madge lived. There were only 3 weeks difference between our ages, and we were both 4 years old at the time. I don't remember granddad Hagger because he was always away on the railroad where he worked. Also living with granny were, Madge's mother, Aunt Ethel, Aunt Ella, Aunt Alice, and the boys, Richard (Dicky) and Herbert (Bunny)

I recall the day we traveled on a bus from Lincoln Flats to Hull for a visit with Granny Hagger. I think I must have driven my mother crazy asking, "are we nearly there, is it much further?" It was a long way from Lincoln Flats to Hull. I don't remember arriving, but I do remember the day Teddy was born. Madge and I were sent to play in the playhouse out back, Aunt Ehtel brought us our lunch, and we had a great time eating, and playing house with our dolls. Finally Aunt Ethel called us to come inside. We gathered our toys and ran in the house. She informed me that I had a baby brother brought by the doctor in his 'Black Bag.'

I went upstairs where Teddy was lying on my mother's arm. I planked myself on the bed beside them and plainly remember saying to mother, "Look at me as well as him," "I can't look at both of you at the same time," mother said. "Well," I said, "you can look at me with one eye and him with the other." I wonder why that is so prevalent in my memory since that is all I remember; maybe I was a little jealous. He was named Albert Edward Hagger. He was always Teddy, until manhood and he changed his name to Ted. I was in 2nd grade at school when I gave him a special name, **'Albert Edward Christian George Andrew Patrick David.'** I assured him that this was his real name. I taught it to him, making sure he memorized it completely. It was actually the name of The Prince of Wales. We had to learn it in class at school, and since Teddy was too young to attend school; it was my belief that if I had to learn it then so should he.

(Years later, in 1974 when I was visiting England, Ted, Joyce and I were traveling in the car, Ted was driving and he was teasing me about something, so I just said "OK Albert Edward Christian George Andrew Patrick David." I thought he was going to stop the car. With a look of surprise he looked at me and said, "That's where I got my name! I always knew it was my name, but I didn't know how I got it." We had quite a discussion about it. I felt a little proud to think of what I had accomplished. Sad to say that being 4 years younger than me when we were separated, that was about all he could remember about me, more about this later).

Life was good at Lincoln Flats; I can well remember the day we moved there as mentioned previously,

The house was what we would call a double here in the States. The back yard was closed in and a brick wall separated us from the yard next door. I recall I had a rather large doll pram and one sunny day unbeknownst to mother, I had put Teddy in the pram and was giving him a ride up and down the walk way when the pram tipped over, I did howl, and had some badly scraped knuckles. My punishment as usual was being sent to bed. I got the worst of it; Teddy was fine with no cuts or bruises.   I really did love him and we had lots of fun during the remainder of our short time together

I remember my first china doll; its eyes would open and close. One day I arrived home from school to find that my dear little brother had taken his toy hammer, and smashed my doll's head to see what made its eyes open and close. Another problem was once when we had been to the seaside at Bridlington, and brought back our buckets and spades, which were great for playing in the garden. I clearly explained to him that being younger than me, he must have a wooden spade. He just didn't see it my way at all, he proceeded to take it away from me and hit me over the top of my eyebrow. Since there was no doctor close to Lincoln Flats, mother took me to the Chemist. I still have the scar to prove it, which left me with barely a half of my left eyebrow.

However, there were many good days, Teddy loved to ride on the back of my bicycle. He had a pet pig named Billy; dad had bought it cheap as it was the runt of the litter and Teddy claimed it as his. They would romp together along the garden path and Billy would run ahead of Teddy, and then come to a sudden stop and Teddy would fall over him and they would both squeal.

I became acquainted with Barbara and Mary Bratley, twins at a nearby farm. We had fun playing on the Mile Pond close by when it froze over. The pond was said to be a mile deep. Shortly after our move to Lincoln Flats, Mrs. Cook and her two fourteen year old twin sons Ivor and Herbert moved in next door. Ivor walked the twins and me to school each morning and met us after school to walk us home. We were sad when they were sent away to naval school. (Sad to say they both insisted on being on the same ship during the war, and were torpedoed and lost at sea.) One day my mother's favorite brother Uncle Ernie and wife, Auntie Amy, came to visit on their motorbike and sidecar. They didn't have any children and asked if they could take me home with them for a visit. It was great fun riding in the sidecar with Auntie Amy, but I can't remember how long I stayed; they owned a fish and chip shop. The name of their house was Melrose. Thanks to Dolly, never again did I stay overnight with them. Soon after I returned home from my visit, she told me that Uncle Ernie and Auntie Amy's house was haunted.

I attended school from Infants through second grade at Foggathorpe; Miss Bielby was the teacher of two classes, the infant's class and grade one. (She was the best teacher I ever had.) One year during second grade, She directed the play 'The Sleeping Beauty. The entire school had a part, and it was a smashing success. Later, we had a garden party and she wrote a song about the Squire of Foggathorpe. It went like this

Our young Squire here at Foggathorpe

He has a streamlined auto

He does his eighty miles an hour

Which is faster than he oughta.

Funny, how some things stick in our memories. Miss Loftus was the Head Mistress of the school and taught grades two through seventh. There was a small shop in Foggathorpe owned by Mr. and Mrs. Alden. They owned a huge rocking horse, located in a room at the back of their shop.

After school, we were allowed to stop, and have a ride on the horse. We spent many happy hours taking turns riding the horse. Dolly and Billy, my uncle and aunt lived with us for a time. Billy taught me to count and say my ABC's. Dolly was only 7 years older than me, and was more like my sister than my aunt. That was a happy time of my life. I was very close to my dad. (I always think of him as my real dad) sometimes when he was visiting neighbors, he would take me with him, riding me on the handlebars of his bike.

One Saturday mother went to York, to do some shopping. While she was gone my dad entertained me with stories, then I sat on his knee and tried to teach him to knit. He was a very patient person; mother was quite upset because I was not in bed when she arrived home. Christmas was a lovely time of the year especially at school. About 3 weeks before Christmas, during class we would write a letter to Father Christmas; (our American Santa Claus,) shortly before Christmas a tree was put up and decorated. There was a partition between the two rooms, that would slide open to make one large room. A few days before Christmas a party would be planned for us, and Father Christmas would arrive with the presents we had asked for in our letters.

I attended Sunday school at the Foggathorpe Methodist chapel every Sunday. For the yearly Sunday School Anniversary we always had to memorize a recitation to say during the service. One-year aunt Ethel, Madge's mother, made lovely dresses for Madge and me, so that we would be dressed alike when we attended the Anniversary Service. The dresses were made of a cream colored net material with frills that were embroidered with forget-me-knots. We loved those dresses and wore them with great pride. I loved it when on some Sundays Mother and dad would take me walking through the Bluebell woods. We would watch the squirrels as the gathered acorns, while we were picking bluebells, the beautiful blue wildflowers.

Sometimes on Sunday afternoons we would ride our bicycles to the village of Nunburnum. I can't remember whom we visited but I do remember they had the most beautiful rhododendrons in their back yard. Those were some of the best years of my life in England. It was while I was still in second grade that mother become ill, and was taken to hospital. I don't remember who took us, but I do remember that I went into the hospital. I wasn't supposed to be there and whoever was in charge of me was told to get me out of there. It must have been my mother's friend Beatty Jackson, because I was taken to her house at Nayburn Rd, near York. I always knew her as Auntie Beatty; I stayed there until mother was back home.

I must have been there quite a long time, because I attended school at Fulford near York. I assumed Teddy would be staying with Granny Hagger and family. I really liked Fulford School, especially because we had hot lunches served to us every day. I made quite a few friends and one boy in particular. I loved walking along the lane that went toward Nayburn. All along the way each side of the road was covered with violets and they were a lovely sight. Auntie Beatty was very strict but I didn't mind. She was housekeeper for Mr. Bannister who had a son named Jimmy. He was 2 years younger than me. We became good friends and played well together.

One day Auntie Beatty sent Jimmy and me on an errand to Nayburn. She gave us strict orders to come straight home, be sure to stay away from the railroad station, and stay off the railroad tracks. Needless to say we spent most of our time playing on the tracks. On the way back as we came in sight of the house, there stood Aunt Beatty in the middle of the road waiting for us, we looked at each other and frowned, we knew we were in trouble. We both received a good talking to and a not so good spanking. We wondered how she knew we had been on the tracks. She never told us and we didn't ask. We decided someone who knew us had seen us and told her; needless to say, we were never allowed to go on any more errands.

I Remember being there during Easter, we were given Easter eggs and while we were still in our pajamas, we were allowed to play till breakfast was ready, the front hall was large and the floor was covered with linoleum and was very shiny and slippery, and Jimmy and I still in pajamas and sock feet, were having a rare old time sliding on the floor when I fell on my face and cut my chin. I did make a noise crying, Aunt Beatty dressed the cut, pulled it together and put a band-aid on it. I till have a faint scar. Apart from the one minor accident I enjoyed staying there. I loved the walks through the fields to friend's homes. We would play marbles with the children while there, such good memories. Finally, Mother was released from the hospital, and I was back home again. Back at Lincoln Flats and Foggathorpe School.

We had a little dog, a white Pomeranian named Pat, and she had a lovely long white tail. She followed me to school one day and Miss Loftus let her stay inside until she decided she had been still long enough, and Miss Loftus made me take her out and send her home. She would always meet me at the corner of the street where the school was located, mother said she knew the exact time to leave home to be at the corner when school was dismissed; and she would be standing there waiting for me.

She was a very smart dog but she hated washdays and always hid, because she knew that it was her bath time. Mother would finally find her, and after she had her bath she would run to the orchard and roll over and over in the grass. When she was outside she would watch the railroad, and was a terror for chasing the trains. One day she had been chasing a train, and began howling, and ran to the front door. Mother took her inside, then went and sat in a chair. Pat ran around the room, and then jumped on mother's knee. Mother looked down, and saw that there was blood on her apron. Pat had lost her beautiful tail to the train. Needless to say it didn't stop her from chasing the trains.

We had new neighbors next door I can't remember their names, but they had a little girl named Mary, the same age as Teddy, they could play together through the fence, Mary's mother wouldn't allow Mary on our side of the fence and she didn't allow Teddy on Mary's side; they were strange people. We never even knew their names. One day as the nine o'clock express train was due to pass through the gates, the husband didn't get to the gates in time, the train hit the gates and he was knocked unconscious. There was no doctor nearby, no phones, and no busses.

The nearest doctor was at Holme on Spalding Moore, about 4 miles from Lincoln Flats. Mother offered to walk to Holme to get the doctor and asked if Teddy and I could stay with the man's wife. She said she could only take Teddy, so I had to stay by myself.

I wasn't at school as it was summer holidays. I thought my mother was never going to get back. Guess I was about seven at the time. I can't remember if she rode home with the doctor or if she walked back. That was the end of the neighbors, they moved away and we never heard how the man was or if he recovered.

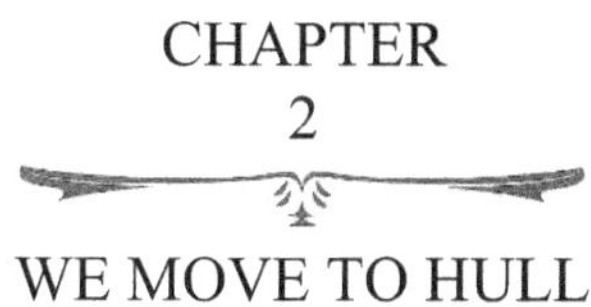

CHAPTER
2

WE MOVE TO HULL

JANUARY 1936

King George the V died; a short time later we left Lincoln Flats. I guess it was because of the depression that times were pretty hard. There was not much work for men except on the farms at very low pay. Mother used to help by working in the farmer's fields picking peas. Teddy and I always went along with her. Most of the other women who worked there also had their children with them. The ones of us who were old enough would help with the picking until we tired of it. We would then all get together and play while the women worked. We had coal fires and coal was scarce and very expensive.

To find greener pastures mother and dad decided to move to Hull. We said goodbye to Lincoln Flats, a very sad day for me; It meant a new school to get used to. As near as I can remember I was almost nine, and Teddy would have been almost five. I was unhappy at the time but after thinking it over, I thought that it wouldn't be so bad, because now that we had moved to Hull I was living close to my cousin Madge, we were able to play together after school. I really enjoyed my new school, and I made new friends.

MY SUMMER VISIT TO THE FARM

During summer holidays I decided I wanted to visit Granny and Granddad Lincoln. They now had a different farm called 'Peters Field' near Everingham E. Yorkshire. I was excited because I would see Dolly. Granny was not very tall; she looked much heavier that she really was due to the fact that she wore so many clothes. She was always complaining about her 'rheumatics' sometimes she was disagreeable, cross, bad tempered and just plain crabby. This sounds disrespectful, but that was just the way she was. I always supposed it was because she was totally deaf in one ear and hard of hearing in the other ear.

We had to shout in order to make her hear us. She was not a very pleasant person. If she saw us laughing she sometimes imagined we were making fun of her. Granddad's personality was just the opposite; he was a jolly old gentleman with a big round tummy and a walrus moustache. I loved it when he would play what he called his melodeon (resembling an accordion with about fifteen buttons on one side and no keys on the other side) Sometimes granddad would dance as he played while granny muttered and complained.

Granddad did a lot of the farm work himself, but he had laborers to help with milking the cows, tending the sheep, horses, pigs, chickens, and all the rest of the work that must be done on a farm. The laborers had living quarters in the back of the house with separate stairs leading to their rooms; they also ate their meals with the family. There was so much work to be done at the farmhouse that granny had to have a maid: cooking was done on a coal stove, there was no electricity, gas, dishwashers, or washing machines and dryers. In addition to daily house cleaning, after the cows were milked, the cream had to be separated, and the cream made into butter.

The separators had to be sterilized, and Granny was always finding fault with the maid's work, she had trouble keeping a maid. I was looking forward to being with Dolly, (as I mentioned earlier I never called her aunt as she was only seven years older than me.) No such luck, not a chance of having fun with her, she wasn't allowed to go out to play; she had to help with the chores. Another maid had left. The weather was lovely that week, and there were lots of fun things to enjoy on the farm. The fields and meadows were carpeted with golden buttercups, and tiny white daisies.

In the orchard the June apples were ripe and just waiting to tempt my taste buds. I loved to swing on the garden gate and look out across the fields where the cows were lazing in the sun, their tails swishing the flies away while the horses and sheep munched away at the juicy green grass. There were lots of buildings and barns to explore, and a lovely pond where I could go and sit idly on the bank and watch the Kingfishers flying and flipping along on top of the water, once in a while a fish would jump up to catch a tasty morsel. I often slipped off my shoes and socks, dipped my feet in the water when it wasn't too cold I would wiggle my toes in the lovely clear water. The nosy ducks would come swimming by to see if my toes were tasty treats.

I had been having such a good time, when one morning as I woke up oohh I felt terrible*!!* I went downstairs and told granny how awful I felt, I was aching all over I just wanted to go back to bed. THAT WAS AGAINST ALL RULES AND REGULATIONS! I couldn't eat much breakfast. "Outside you go young lady," granny shouted, as I mentioned before she was very deaf. "But granny," I whimpered, trying to make her hear, I feel so poorly (our British way of saying I feel so sick) She opened the door and practically pushed me outside, then slammed the door shut as she went back inside. I leaned on the door, crying, thinking, *"Oh how I wished I were home with my mother."* I opened the door and peeped in the kitchen, Dolly was washing the dishes because as usual there was no maid, poor Dolly had all the extra work to do, quite a task for a fifteen year old. "Please ask her to let me in Dolly*,"* I pleaded. "Kath," she said, " I can't ask her for anything, because she will only box my ears for asking."

Granny marched into the kitchen, "Now what do you want?" she growled. "Oh dear," I moaned. "What's that? Speak up and stop your whining," she said, I begged and pleaded, raising my voice to make her hear, "Please Granny, let me come in I feel so bad" I began to cry. She pushed me outside "You are whining crybaby, why can't you be like Alan *' (my cousin) '*he was here last summer and he was good little lad he wasn't a bit of trouble, why can't you be like him." That really helped my feeling of inferiority! By this time I was really crying and sobbing, she grabbed hold of me and said, "Let me look at you!" She felt my forehead. "Just as I thought, you have a fever," she grumbled as she lifted my dress and looked at my tummy.

"You have the measles." now she was really furious. "Your mother knew you were coming down with them and wanted rid of you," she shouted. I felt so miserably ill, unloved, and unwanted. Wiping my tears I thought, "If she would only let me go to bed." But no! Granny had other plans. Grumbling and complaining about mothers not wanting to take care of their own children, gritting her teeth she said, "I'm packing you off home my lady." Dolly was feeling sorry for me and knowing that Granny couldn't hear what she was saying, she put her arms around me trying her best to comfort me.

"You get her ready," granny told Dolly. "Take her to the bus stop and see that she gets on the bus." It was about two miles to the nearest bus stop, which was on the road to Market Weighton. Dolly packed my suitcase, put me on the seat of her bicycle, and pushed me to the bus stop. The bus driver knew Dolly and my mother, he told us that he was going to the garage in Hull where I lived, then asked." If I take you to the end of your street can you find your house?" I told him I could. I finally arrived home, mother put me to bed, and I never saw granny anymore till I was fourteen. I finally recovered from the measles and life went on.

MY WORLD FELL APART

It was just after my ninth birthday, it was a lovely day, I came home from school with not a care in the world, and I went skipping into the apartment that we had recently moved into. My mother called to me, "I want to talk to you Kathleen," she said. I sat on the table on the back kitchen, the table was used for scrubbing dirty clothes on washdays I was swinging my legs, and humming a happy tune, wondering what she was going to talk about. That's when my world went crashing around me, unforgotten words from my mother, "I am leaving your dad, she said, and because you, being a girl, and the oldest, must choose, I can't have both you and Teddy, you must decide; do you want to go with me or stay with your dad?" I was flabbergasted! I had no idea that there were any problems between them. I said, "Of course I want to be with you mother;"(*Except for one time about a week later that was the last time I saw my brother Teddy until 1960 he was thirty years old; I was thirty four)*

So began my new life as Kathleen Marshall. It was the beginning of my introverted, poor self-image. I always felt that my mother would rather have been able to take Teddy, I saw her crying so many times and heard her tell my stepfather she wished she could see Teddy. I couldn't talk to my mother about how I felt. I just kept it all my inside. I felt lost without Teddy and my dad. My stepfather was Ted Marshall, I was very unhappy. The place where we went to live was unbelievable, located in Lincolnshire, at a small farm in a valley called Deep Dale. It was situated between two hills. At the bottom of the hills were a small Chapel, and two houses. Across the road from the Chapel was a dirt road that went across two fields, ending at a large farmhouse, occupied by Mr. Osgerby and his family. This whole area was a part of the estate of a well to do farmer, Mr. Golland. He owned thousands of acres of farmland, including all the above land, and buildings, including the place we were going to move into. Mr. Osgerby was the foreman of the estate and all tenants living on the estate, including Ted, were employees.

The house where we were to live had three bedrooms, living room, and kitchen. It was a brick cottage along with several outbuildings, a barn, and small orchard. The only way to reach this place from the main road, was to first go down the dirt road to the foreman's farm, then crossing a meadow. From the meadow, to a dirt rutted cart road that was the length of two fields, and ended at a wheat field, across the middle of which a pathway was trodden. Finally ending up at what was called 'Little Deep Dale.' The worst was yet to come! We moved in and it didn't look too bad from the outside, but when we went upstairs—what a shock! As I walked into what was to be my bedroom my legs were covered with fleas. I was screaming, running, jumping, and crying. I often wonder how my mother felt about such an upheaval. She told Ted we couldn't sleep with such a mess. He had to go somewhere to buy something that would get rid of the fleas in a hurry. There were no buses, or any roads. It was three miles across more fields to the nearest town, Barton on Humber. As he left, we watched him walk across the first field then disappear from view.

It was hours before he returned. Even though he did his best to rid us of the interlopers, it took a long frustrating amount of time to finally be free of them. When washday came I wasn't very happy, watching mother wash our bed linens. The stains from the fleas were hard to deal with. I saw her crying and wished she would go back to my dad and Teddy. I wondered why in the world had Ted brought us to such a place, so far from our beloved Yorkshire. The only way back to Hull was by ferry, across the River Humber from the village of New Holland. I didn't realize at the time that I wouldn't see Teddy any more till 1960 and Madge till the year 1974 I cried a lot and I saw mother sometimes crying because she had left Teddy. I wished we could go back to Hull to dad and Teddy. I could never bring myself to talk to my mother about how I felt. Maybe if she had been a more affectionate person I would have felt different. I don't mean she didn't love me; I know she did, she just never told me, or showed me. (*I go overboard making sure my children know I love them*)

I finally became friends with the Osgerby children at the foreman's farm; we had great fun playing in the fields and around the barnyard. At harvest time, we would often take drinks and food to the workers. Thank goodness there was a bus to take us to Barton School. I would walk across the fields each morning and join the Osgerby children at the main road in front of the Chapel There the bus would pick us up after a very long walk. I really liked the school and became friends with Sheila Mellars. At this time I was in the fourth grade. Sometimes on weekends, I would be invited to spend time at Sheila's home. And sometimes after School, she would ride on the school bus with me and stay all night at my home. The next morning we were able to travel to school together. After school she would go back home. She taught me to play draughts (checkers in America.)

Shortly after my tenth birthday September sixth 1936, mother had to be taken to the hospital. I stayed at the Osgerby farm and I thought she was never coming back; she was in hospital several weeks. When she finally came home, she brought with her my baby brother, named James Edwin, which became shortened to Jimmy. I finally put aside a lot of my bad feelings toward my stepfather, but I always called him Ted. He didn't adopt me, but I lived under the name of Marshall from then on. Jimmy made a big difference in my outlook on life, but I would often see my mother crying, and I couldn't tell her how I felt but I used to think that she wished she had Teddy instead of me. I always thought about it but never could tell anyone my feelings. Jimmy took so much of our time. During the first weeks of his life, Jimmy slept most of the day and cried most of the night. Finally, he had his days and nights back in the right order, I loved helping take care of him, he was a little imp but I loved him. When he was two years old, I wrote two stories about him.

HAPPY DAY! WE LEAVE LITTLE DEEP DALE.

About a year later, we moved to the village of Barrow on Humber, to a lovely clean house with a long hall from the front door to the stairs, upstairs three bedrooms. Downstairs a living room, three steps up to the kitchen and a small hall to the back door. There was a lovely back yard with a garden, a lovely orange blossom tree, and an apple tree. Best of all it only took ten minutes to walk to school. Another school to get used to, but this time quite different from the previous Council Schools I had attended. The Barrow on Humber Church of England School, it was the only school in Barrow therefore it was the public school. Infants (Kindergarten) had their own separate area for class and playground. Every morning when the bell rang, all classes met in the hall for assembly. The meeting opened with everyone repeating The Lord's Prayer, followed by singing a hymn. Then marching to our individual class-room for lessons. The first lesson consisted of reading from the Bible, also learning The Apostles Creed. This was actually the last school I attended. I was in the seventh grade for two semesters. It was mandatory that we go until the age of fourteen. . What a joy it was to be able to walk to school and it only took ten minutes.

1938

Mother was a terrific cook; she and Ted talked this over and decided she would bake a number of breads, cakes, pies, and other desserts. Ted would put everything in baskets, and take the goodies around the neighborhood to sell them. It was so successful they decided to make plans for opening a bakery. It was during this time that Ted called upon a family Ernie and Jessie Reynolds who became great friends. Later, Jessie becomes a part of my story. Mother became very ill and visited the doctor. He told her she was pregnant, she was so ill she wasn't able to continue baking. It was so sad, the bakery plans had to be scratched. Ted had to visit his regular customers and cancel orders. It must have been quite a disappointment; he had a large number of regular customers.

Raymond was born June 18th.1938, he was a lovely chubby baby and so cute. Now I had two little brothers to baby sit. Ted called him 'Little Podgy,' Jimmy couldn't say Podgy, he said 'Poggy,' and until he died, Raymond always went by the name Poggy. We moved again, thankfully it was located in the same village. It was a small farm with five acres of land consisting of a large orchard of pear, apple, and plum trees; also raspberry and gooseberry bushes. There were two fields, in one field Ted built a large chicken house, and then bought lots of chickens. He rented the other field to another farmer who needed a place to pasture his sheep. Ted bought some pigs, one was a big sow named Phyllis on who's back Jimmy learned to ride.

There were several outbuildings and a barn, also a washhouse in the back yard. The house had three bedrooms, a living room, kitchen, and scullery. This was one of the best homes we had lived in and it wasn't much further to walk to school. It certainly was a great place for Jimmy to play. My friends loved to visit after school. Jimmy had a time trying to pronounce my name and to him I was always Kak. At bedtime he always wanted to hold my thumb to rub his nose with it, if I refused he would shout "Mummy, Kak won't hold me tum." Actually it was my thumb he was holding. Mother would respond, "Kak hold Jimmy's tum." These were just a few of Jimmy's escapades; he was almost three years old at the time, and he could always be found following his dad. He was a little terror, always causing trouble for me. Especially on Saturdays, when Mother and Ted would go to the market, and I always had to take care of Jimmy while they were gone. He always got into mischief, for instance; one Saturday when they had gone to market, and as usual I had to watch him. I was an avid reader and lost myself in my book at times.

There were ten sittings of eggs in the barn, some of them were in orange crates, and one was in a small dishpan. Before they left Ted said; "Kath, be sure and watch Jimmy. Don't let him go in the barn, because the hens will peck at him and he could be badly hurt." I really did watch him for a long time, and because he was happily playing in the orchard, I told him to stay away from the barn; then went inside, picked up my book and had a good read, when it was almost time for mother and Ted to come home, I gave Jimmy a bath and put clean clothes on him. I felt I had done a good job. Mother thanked me for having him all nice and clean.

While she was fixing dinner and Ted went out to take care of the livestock with Jimmy at his heels. All of a sudden we heard Ted give out a yell, he was shouting and yelling at Jimmy. Mother and I went running to the barn to see what was happening. We arrived on the scene and-- OH MY, Jimmy had taken every one of the eggs from the orange crates and piled them on the small dish pan, and all the hens were fighting to get on the dish pan. I wanted to run and hide, It was a wonder the hens hadn't pecked him to pieces. I often wonder what was going through his mind when he was moving the eggs. Needless to say my books were off limit to me for quite some time.

Mondays were always washing days; in those days there were no washing machines or dryers. Out back there was a wash house that had a copper, the best way I can describe it is a large stone bowl under which a fire would be built; then it would be filled with water, and after washing things in a tub with a wash board and a gadget called a posher that had a long handle, and at the bottom of the handle was a round object with a cup like shape. It was bounced up and down on the clothes in the soapy water, and then the white things such as sheets tablecloths etc. were transferred to the copper to be boiled, then transferred to a tub of clear water, to which was added a blue substance for rinsing. Then they went through the wringer and hung out to dry. Almost unimaginable in this day and time

On one washday mother said she was busy with the washing, and Jimmy came running out of the house he was so excited "Mummy, Mummy," he squealed, "he's gone Mummy, he's gone." Who's gone?" mother asked. "Jackie's gone,' yelled Jimmy. "Where has he gone?" asked mother." I wet him fwy away wid dem udder widdle dicky birds." Jackie was our little green parakeet. Needless to say we never did find him. Another time she said she heard the kitten wailing, and ran out to find he had washed the kitten, and was trying to put her through the wringer. Thank goodness the kitten wasn't hurt.

An elderly seaman friend of the family, wrote a poem about Jimmy, it goes like this-

If you go to Barrow there you will see

A sailor boy named Jimmy,

Who never goes to sea?

Of all the seas he sailed in

Wouldn't drown a mouse

Cause you'll always find him sailing

Round his daddy's chicken house

I loved this home, I loved going to the fields gathering flowers, violets, primroses buttercups, daises, and cowslips. Nowhere have I ever found such lovely flowers as grow wild in England. I enjoyed going for walks taking Poggy out in the pram, I liked the school at Barrow, I made quite a number of friends who enjoyed visiting our home as there was a lot of room to play in the out buildings and fields around us. I became acquainted with Ted's sister Lillian otherwise known as Aunt Lil. She was very special to me; she had three children, Betty older than me, Sammy, who was my age, and the youngest Rosy. I spent some time with them on holidays. Aunt Lil as I called her and Betty worked as ushers at a local theater. I got a lot of Betty's hand me down clothes. One coat, was a winter coat that had belonged to Betty, it became my favorite coat.

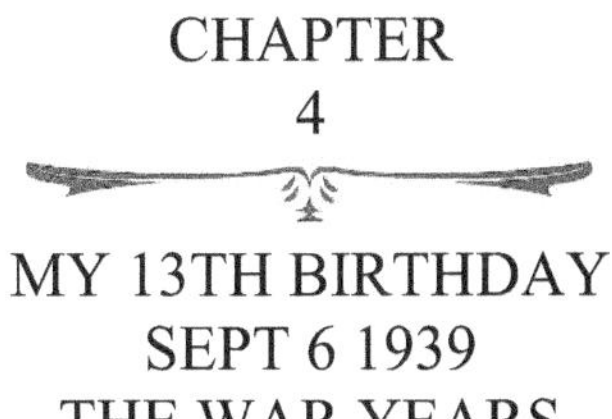

CHAPTER
4

MY 13TH BIRTHDAY
SEPT 6 1939
THE WAR YEARS

Friday Sept 1st 1939 I went to New Holland, I boarded the ferry to Hull, and I went to all the schools I could reach that day. The schools were evacuating children from Hull to the countryside. I was looking for Teddy, assuming he would be evacuated. Hull being a large seaport had a lot of schools in the area where I thought Teddy might attend. There were large groups of children lined up at each school, waiting for buses to take them to different homes in villages. I returned to the ferry, tired and sad because I didn't find him. Many changes came because of the war. Everyone had to become registered by the government. Identification numbers were given to us, and then we were given ration books. I have never forgotten our numbers, Ted's was TNGN 151 then mother's TNGN 152, mine was 153, Jimmy's 154, Raymond's 155, and later, Michael's 156. Clothes (except shoes) were rationed, and all food was rationed (except bread.) No one was allowed oranges, or bananas, (except pregnant women).

The first time we heard the air raid sirens we were all afraid, but the air raids didn't reach this far north until later. The Germans were concentrating on London. Michael was born on October 31st. 1939. The doctor had to be brought in; we thought we were going to lose mother. The doctor told Ted he couldn't save both mother and the baby. Ted had to choose which one he wished the doctor to save. Of course Ted told him to save mother. This was a terrible time of waiting. The doctor did manage to save them both. Michael wasn't at all like Raymond. He was such a tiny baby, but so sweet. This is where (previously mentioned) Auntie Jessie came to our rescue. Every morning after she got her son off to school, she would come on her bicycle to help mother with the chores. Ted was working at a green house in the next village. Now I had three little brothers to baby sit. Michael was named Brian Michael, but was always known as Michael.

The following spring mother became quite ill. She was taken to the Hospital in Scunthorpe, a large town in Lincolnshire. She had gallstones and jaundice and was in hospital for nearly three months. She almost lost her life. Again Aunty Jessie came to take care of the three boys, Jimmy, Raymond, Michael, and me. Ted was working at a farm along with tending to the livestock and garden at home. I went to visit mother at the hospital every weekend. School was interesting; I still had a year to go. Soon after the war began, a group of boys were evacuated to our village of Barrow. We (the village children) went to school in the mornings and the evacuees went in the afternoons. I became acquainted with one of the boys named Frank Galloway; Frank would come over after school. One day he let all the little pigs out of the sty and they ran in a wheat field. I was afraid Ted would be home from work before we got them rounded up and back in the sty. Thank goodness we made it in time.

Another day Frank climbed on top of our outside toilet, it was brick with a tile roof. He fell through the roof. I thought 'now I will catch it when Ted gets home and sees the hole in the roof of the toilet.' I didn't say anything about it after he came home, but I was holding my breath while he was feeding the chickens and pigs and tending to his chores, but he never said anything, I breathed a sigh of relief, safe for the time being! That night the air raid warning sounded and we could hear distant gunfire, but nothing that sounded really close. The next morning after Ted took care of the livestock, he came in and said (Yorkshire language) "By Gum Kath, The Jerries (Germans) must have been closer than we thought last night, there's a big hole in the roof of the toilet." "Really," I said, "They didn't sound that close." Wow saved by the Jerries! (He never knew till 1960 when I had to take a trip home, I finally confessed and we had a good laugh.)

My mother finally came home from the hospital, and now due to the war, Ted was called into the army. That would leave five of us when he left, mother, Jimmy, Raymond, Michael, and me. We had to sell everything on our small farm. Ted got an extended leave from the army in order to move us to Sutton on Sea. (Because mother was still very weak, Aunty Jessie went with us to help.) I loved Sutton on Sea. My friend Joan went with us for a holiday. There was an air base close to our house. It was a Spitfire Base. At that time England was expecting an invasion by the

Germans. Armed Guards were posted all around the villages and the sands at the seaside were all covered with barbed wire, and no one was allowed on the sands. One day Joan had taken Michael outside for a walk in his stroller. She came running in, "Mrs. Marshall," she cried, "bombs are dropping from a plane in the sky." We went running out to see what was happening, and way off in the distance a German plane had been shot down by a spitfire. What Joan thought were bombs, was actually the German pilot and crew jumping out of the plane and parachuting to the ground. Life was very frightening back then. Close to where we lived a large mansion was being used, to house the airmen from the Spitfire Base.

1940

I went on my first date for my fourteenth birthday; a sixteen-year-old boy named Alan took me to the village of Mablethorpe to see a movie, we went on mother's tandem. I was really disappointed when mother decided to move back to Barrow because she missed her old friends; so back to Barrow we went. Around this time Jimmy came down with scarlet fever. He was taken to the hospital, where he was quarantined for six weeks No one was allowed to see him except mother, She could only see him through a glass window on visiting days. He came home after the six weeks, a changed little boy. Still mischievous but not the boisterous child anymore, he was very clever because he could interpret Michael's vocabulary. When Michael was upset by not being understood, and if Jimmy was nearby, we would ask him to please tell us what Michael was trying to say?" Jimmy would have a short conversation with Michael, after listening to his answer Jimmy would then tell us what it was that Michael wanted, and it always satisfied Michael.

I was almost fifteen, when I worked as maid for Lady Brocklesby. Her husband, Mr. Golland was the same farmer who owned Deep Dale. Lady Brocklesby was his wife. They had a lovely home on a beautiful area on top of a hill with an awesome view, but the water had to be pumped from a well into a huge holding tank, in order to have running water in the house. It was my job to pump it in the evening, and I used to think I would never get the tank full. I wasn't happy there, at night there were air raids at Grimsby about 25 miles away, I could hear the anti-aircraft guns and the explosions from the bombs and I was afraid. I always prayed during air raids asking God to not let me die. I never told anyone how afraid I was. Lady Brocklesby was very kind to me; she did a lot of her own work such as canning tomatoes. She taught me how to scald them in order to remove the peel. She also taught me how to set a dinner table, including how to arrange the silverware, sometimes at dinner time there would be twelve people around the table. I also took Baby Martin out for walks in his pram. I was very homesick, I finally left, and went back home, and for a while I worked on a farm, and one of the farm hands taught me to drive the tractor.

Meanwhile the Nazis blitzed Hull, being a Sea Port, the docks were heavily bombed, I would venture to say by the end of the war there wasn't a street in Hull that hadn't been bombed. It was a terrible time. Debris from the raids was blown across the River Humber, and landed in New Holland from where the ferryboat traveled. I worked on the farm for quite some time, then mother and I had words over something, I don't remember what it was about, and because the air raids seemed to be fewer at Hull, I decided I would go there and stay with a friend, Nelly Boswell.

1941

By this time I was fifteen, and I began working at the pickle factory. I got quite a surprise to find that the Germans were still visiting Hull with their loads of bombs. We spent most nights in the air raid shelters. As the planes were approaching, we could tell they were loaded with bombs by their laboring sound. As they were arrived overhead the bombs would begin falling; and I would silently pray my usual prayer. "Please God, don't let me die, don't let the bombs hit us," I was so afraid, there were several others in the shelter, and as we listened to the screaming noise of the falling bombs some children would be crying. The adults would be trying to stay calm, but most of us were holding our breath until the bombs landed, and we heard the explosion. How I still thank the Lord for keeping us safe.

Sometimes a friend and I would go out after a raid to see what the damage was. There would be bricks and glass all over the streets, people were crying, the ambulances were there, and some people were being dug out of the piles and piles of bricks and furniture, or what was left of the demolished houses. One night we walked toward the docks and there were fires blazing everywhere. It looked like the entire docks were on fire. Because it was so bad in Hull, I finally decided to go back home to mother and the boys. A surprise awaited me at Barrow; while I was away there had been a bad air raid. Mother informed me that a widow, Doris Jones along with her two children, Gwen, who was my age, and four year old Roy; were living with us. Their next door neighbor had suffered a direct hit by a bomb, and the Jones family having been hiding in a closet under their stairs were buried for hours in the tiny room, calling for help until they were found, and rescued. Both houses were demolished. In the house where the bomb hit, eighteen-year-old Pearl Tong and her mother were killed; Mr. Tong was out on Home Guard duty during the raid and was spared.

A young man found pieces of Pearl's body across the street from where the family had lived. Their   bed-clothes were blown onto the roof our house, which was about two blocks away. . Our house was brick, and when the bomb exploded the results of the explosion shook our house so hard it shook the plaster from the ceilings in our upstairs bedrooms. Our beds had to be brought down; we could no longer use the upstairs. The Jones family lived with us quite a while, because there was no other place available It was a usual occurrence those days when someone was bombed out of his or her home, families would take them in and care for them. There were more air raids on Barrow, because the raiders were evidently trying to hit the ammunition dump in the area.

The Germans had a radio program every night with a person named Lord Haw, Haw. One night he made the announcement that they knew where the Ammunition Dump was in Barrow Haven, and sure enough there was a raid the following night, but they never succeeded in hitting it. One morning as I opened the front door after a night of air raids, I started to step outside but stopped in horror, there was an incendiary bomb on our doorstep, and it hadn't exploded. I stepped over it and since we had no phone, I ran to the fire department for help. The firemen came to remove it, and once again we were kept safe.

Life went on I would soon be sixteen, and I went to work on the farm down the road. Then one day Mother finally decided it was time to get in touch with Auntie Dora and Dolly. So she wrote to Auntie Dora and asked if she and Dolly would like to meet mother and me at Paragon Station in Hull, we soon had an answer back asking us to meet them at a certain time at the station. Mother and I met them as planned, what a reunion it was after all these years. We were soon spending lots of weekends with Dolly, she and her husband Matt had a farm called Forest Farm at Holme on Spalding Moore on the Yorkshire Dales. The Royal Air Force had taken possession of the land nearby, and there were Nisson Huts all around in the woods. The lane we had to travel to get to and from the Farm, had guards stationed at the end of the lane, and whenever we went out and came back in we were asked "who goes there" and we had to answer "Friend" and they would check us and let us go through.

Granny and Granddad Lincoln lived with Dolly and Matt, Granddad had to give up farming; he was kicked by a horse and was in hospital for a year. He was left with a lame leg. Some of the airmen would visit and play darts with granddad. Those were happy days. Our three boys were little rascals, Jimmy and Dot, (Dolly's daughter) were the same age, five years old, Raymond was four, and Michael was three. They loved to visit the farm; one Saturday they had been very quiet, we should have known something was amiss. An angry airman came and knocked on the door, asking for Dolly and mother "Where are those children of yours?" he asked. "They are out playing." mother said. "Just come and see what they have done," the airman said. We all followed behind him as he led us to his car. "Just take a good look at it," he said angrily; it was a big mess, because they had whitewashed the entire car. It took a lot of apologizing and cleaning. I really don't remember the outcome .I know Mother and Dolly dealt with the culprits, and mother left and went home with the boys.

I decided that I would stay with Dolly and Matt. I went to work on the land while I was there. I helped Dolly house clean, and helped paper all the rooms. Granny helped with the meals.

She didn't like Matt, which is a long story. Granddad would go for walks every day; he had to use a cane because he was very lame. One day he went out early in the morning and was gone all day. When he didn't come home for dinner or at teatime, everyone was worried. Matt and some of the workmen went out looking for him, when they finally found him, Poor granddad. He had got his foot caught in a rabbit hole and couldn't get it out; he said he had shouted all day until he almost lost his voice. He was a pitiful sight when they got him home; he was so tired he just wanted to go to bed. I stayed with Dolly almost a year and finally decided It was time to go home to Barrow

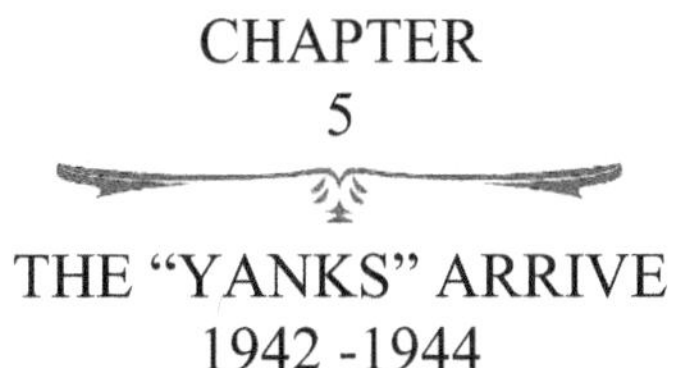

THE "YANKS" ARRIVE
1942 -1944

I was almost sixteen when the American airmen "Yanks" arrived in our quiet little village in Lincolnshire. They came down the main street on their bicycles, and we had never seen or heard any one as rowdy and boisterous. They took our village by storm and headed straight for the Pub, where they proceeded to drink their fill of the warm English beer. I became acquainted with quite a number of them at our local dance hall. Even though I was only sixteen I would pass for eighteen. At Christmas all the American GI's gave up their dinner and took the children of the village to their camp for Christmas dinner. My three brothers, ages three, four, and six, were included, since it was wartime and everything was rationed, it was a real treat for them. They came back loaded with candy, and chewing gum. One day I was working alone for a farmer, out in a field of cabbage plants. I heard the sound of a plane, looked up, and saw an American plane that was flying very low, the pilot was leaning over the side of the plane waving at me, and he came so low I hit the ground. He flew around again and I ducked as he flew by and waved, laughing as he left. I really didn't think it was so funny, as I got to my feet shaking like a leaf.

In the meantime Poggy became very ill, mother called the doctor, he came, and after examining Poggy, diagnosed him with Rheumatic Fever. After giving instructions for Poggy's care, mostly just keep him quiet, and comfortable. A few days later Poggy lost consciousness, It was awful Mother rang the doctor, and before he arrived Poggy had regained consciousness. When he opened his eyes all he said was "Mummy, tell daddy Poggy didn't want to leave Mummy. We were heart broken, Ted was in the far east in the British army, and Poggy often told mother that he would hide in the pantry when daddy came home, and would ask "do you think he will be able to find me?" when the doctor finally arrived he told mother to take Poggy to the hospital as soon as possible, or he wouldn't be responsible for him. The doctor treated mother very coldly, with not a thought of how she was going to get little Poggy to the hospital. (*It is so hard for me to write* *this, after all these years as I am writing, my tears flow,) m*other asked me if I would go to Holme on Spalding Moor to ask Dolly if she would go to Barrow to be with her to help get Poggy to the hospital. There were no hospitals or ambulances anywhere near the village of Barrow, and he would have to be taken to Hull on the ferry. I caught the ferry to Hull, and then took a bus to Holme on Spalding Moor where Dolly lived. When I arrived, I explained what happened to Raymond, and Dolly immediately had a talk with Matt to make sure he approved of her going to mother, of course he was OK with it. Dolly packed in a suitcase, everything she and Dot would need, for a short stay, then prepared to leave with me.

Granny was very angry. As we were getting ready to leave she made a statement that really puzzled me at the time. She told Dolly not to leave with me, because she knew mother just wanted them to get together and have a good time. I tried to convince her that Raymond truly was very ill, the doctor had ordered mother to take him to the hospital, and mother was really upset. I can't begin to tell my feelings as she said; "your mother just wants Dolly there to run around with her, she is no good, it's a wonder she didn't have you in the toilet." I was so upset, but couldn't understand why she would say such a thing; I didn't ask her what she meant, I just wasn't about to let her see me Cry. We left as granny was still muttering and mumbling, we arrived home and as mother was getting Poggy ready to go, a friend who had a large twin pram for her twins, suggested that Mother borrow it in order to take him on the ferry. He was very ill, it was so sad to see them go,

I stayed behind to take care of Jimmy, Michael, and Dot. Mother had to leave Raymond in the hospital, she wasn't allowed to stay, and the last thing she heard as she was escorted out was Raymond crying, "Don't leave me mummy. Our little *"Poggy"* died alone at seven the next morning. *(As I am writing this; after all these years, it still brings tears to my eyes. I can hardly see to write.)* I picked a bunch of violets from the garden, and them put in the casket with him. He was such a sweet child; he had a sunny personality, being so different from his rambunctious brother Jimmy. Some of the Americans sent flowers to the funeral. They had become acquainted with the children in the village and knew Poggy, since he and Jimmy were two of the children joining the GI's for the Christmas dinner

After the funeral we were all sitting around the fire, Dot was deep in thought and she asked mother questions about what had happened to Poggy, mother told her that Jesus had taken him to heaven. Dot thought for a minute and said "Auntie Vi, wouldn't it be awful if a naughty boy would shoot them with a catapult (American sling shot) as Jesus was taking Poggy to heaven." That was a sad time; Ted was in the Far East and was not allowed to come home for the funeral, which made it very hard on mother. Such a tragedy

BACK TO HULL

After the death of Raymond, mother couldn't bear to be in Lincolnshire anymore. We moved back to Hull and were there until I left for America. It took quite a while for Mother to become a little of her old self. A good friend, Blanch Grundy moved in the same Villa just two doors from us; only one side of the villa was left standing, the other side was bombed and nothing was left bit a few bricks. It was good to be back in Hull. There weren't so many air raids by this time. I was now seventeen I began looking for work, and decided to try for employment at Ray Sanderson Oil Mill in Stone Ferry, Hull. I told them I was eighteen and they didn't question me. They were desperate for help since most of the men had been called into Service. I was hired and assigned to a machine with 5 other women. The machine ground large slabs of cattle food into small chunks. . It was very hard work; one person fed the slabs into the machine the chunks came out in two feeders and were caught in sacks. Two women had to lift the filled sack onto a scale, weigh it, then lift it off the scale then two others sewed up the filled sacks and placed each sack on a sack barrow and pushed it to a storage place. We had to have 20 tons ground, bagged, and stored in eight hours each sack weighed 108 lbs. (a British hundred weight)

The first week I was so sore I could hardly move, every bone and muscle in my body ached. It took about two weeks for me to be able to toss the sacks around. We worked alternate weeks one-week six a.m. to two p.m. the following week two p.m. to ten p.m. Summertime afternoon shift wasn't so bad as it stayed daylight till almost 11 p.m. but the mornings I had to leave at five thirty to walk to work and it was dark and no light anywhere unless there was a moon. It was blackout time. It was very scary we weren't allowed to have a flashlight. No light of any kind was allowed. I became friends with Muriel Wilson who was a year or two older than me. Her pet name was Mooey. We became very close, and went everywhere together and were called the "Gold Dust Twins."

One Saturday Mooey, a friend Ginger, and I all decided that we would ride our bicycles to the seaside town of Withernsea. We met at my home at seven a.m. Needless to say, good old British weather as usual, and it was raining. We decided we would take a chance on that old saying: 'Rain before seven fine before eleven' and away we went. We were wearing our Macs and rain scarves. We figured it was about eighteen miles from Hull to Withernsea; (I just looked it up it is seventeen and a half miles) the rain didn't stop by eleven. We kept going till we were soaked and hungry, since we had packed a lunch to take with us we decided we would look for somewhere to stop and eat lunch. We came to an empty cottage and stopped to check it out, it was unlocked, we went inside, there were army cots in one room the rest of the cottage was empty. It appeared to have been a place the army had used at some time. We ate our lunch, and decided that it wasn't going to stop raining, we figured we were only about halfway there, so we mounted our bicycles and started for home, three sad looking soaking wet gals, we never tried it again. There were still a few air raids but not as many or as often until the Germans began flying over the North Sea.

1944

HOW I MET MY FUTURE HUSBAND

One day during a conversation, the subject of Americans came up. Mooey said she had never met a *Yank,* I told her I knew where they hung out, so we made our plans! We had to cross the river Humber by Ferry. It was July eighth 1944. We stopped by a friend's house, and made plans to spend the night, then made our way to the pub called The Six Bells. We entered the lounge, which was like a family gathering room, there was a piano in one corner, and if a musician happened to come in there would be a community sing. To our disappointment, there was no one else there. We ordered a glass of wine; no one questioned my age even though the legal age to enter a pub was eighteen. Mooey hated the name Muriel and informed me, from that time onward she wanted to be known as Sue. (She is still named Sue).

About half an hour passed, when lo and behold, in came two *Yanks*. We began to whisper to each other about how we would gain their attention. It was decided that we would ask if they had any gum. (A favorite expression used was "Got any gum chum")? Now we argued over who would ask. "You ask" said Sue, "you know how to talk to them." We then argued about which one we liked, I said I would only consider it if she would take the one whom we later found out was named Cecil. With this settled, I summoned up the courage to ask the age old question, "Got any gum chum?" The ice was broken; they took the bait! Bill Price was my date; Cecil Neitzel was Sue's date. Bill was from Kentucky, and Cecil was from Iowa. We spent the rest of the evening with them at the Six Bells. It was the law that all pubs closed at ten p.m. After closing time, we went for a walk around the village, and then made a date for the following Saturday, said good night to them, then went to my friend Meg's to spend the night.

I wasn't too impressed with Bill, and when Saturday came, I told Sue I didn't want to keep my date. Sue was upset, called me a spoilsport, and told me if I didn't go she couldn't go alone, and she really wanted to see Cecil. I didn't know it, but my fate was sealed. I gave in, and we returned to Barrow upon Humber, and met Bill and Cecil again. After several dates, I took Bill home to meet my mother. My two little brothers, Jimmy and Michael fell in love with him. Mother finally allowed Bill to spend weekends with us when he could get leave, He always slept in my bedroom, and I slept with mother.

One Saturday night when he was visiting; the air raid warning sounded, mother took Jimmy and Michael to the air raid shelter and told me to wake Bill and then go down to the shelter. I went in the bedroom to wake him. Note that, prior to this the Germans didn't send buzz bombs as far up north as Yorkshire, but now they were in Holland, just across the North Sea. The river Humber ran into the North Sea. I heard a terrible noise at first I thought it was a plane, It was a bright moonlight night so I doused the light, opened the blind and as I looked out of the window I saw this huge flame coming towards us, I jumped on the bed, landing on top of Bill, yelling at the top of my voice, it is one of those things, he pushed me aside, I had scared the daylights out of him. It actually was a buzz bomb as we called them. Needless to say it passed on by, and we joined mother and the boys in the shelter, where we stayed till the all clear sounded. We were told that as long as the buzz bomb could be heard we were safe, but if it suddenly went silent that meant it was coming straight down on us. Very scary, but thank the Good Lord that was the only one that reached our area. Shortly before the war ended we had no more air raids, as soon as planes were sighted on radar, the entire sky surrounding Hull was lit up with thousands of fireworks, no plane could possibly get through them

1945.

Sue and Cecil were married in January. Meanwhile, it was my eighteenth birthday, and on a snowy January afternoon, after Bill had spent the weekend with us; I was seeing him off on the ferry, and as we were gazing out over the river, waiting for the ferryboat to arrive, Bill asked me if I would like to go home with him. Thinking he meant back to camp. I said, "Don't be silly, I can't go to camp with you." "No," he said, "I mean to Kentucky." I told him I would have to think about it. When I told my mother, she was really upset, and said she would forbid it as I was underage, and even though she had come to like Bill, she felt it was too big a step for me to take to go four thousand miles from home. We had a terrible falling out. I have been sorry many times for the way I talked to my mother. She wrote to my stepfather, who was still in the Far East with the British Army. He wrote back and advised her to give her consent, since I was so determined.

By the end of January, Bill was sent to the south of England, to France and then on to Germany. We wrote to each other, He sent me a bottle of French perfume from France, I had never had really French perfume, and I have never had any since. It was absolutely the greatest. One day I arrived home from work, and oh the aroma when I opened the front door, I yelled for Michael, I just knew he had been in my perfume. I knew the culprit couldn't have been Jimmy, since at that time Jimmy was attending school. When I found Michael he had on his over coat, on which he had poured the whole bottle of perfume. I yelled at him and mother yelled at me; telling me not to touch him. I was so upset at the time, but later I was glad I didn't touch him, he was such a cute little guy (little did I know that the week before Bill and I were married he'd be in the hospital.) Bill and I kept up our correspondence until the war between England and Germany ended.

MORE HEARTACHE FOR MOTHER

July sixteenth 1945 Michael was diagnosed with Rheumatic fever and admitted to Sutton Hospital. Terrible news, we thought about what happened to Raymond and hoped and prayed we wouldn't also lose Michael. On Saturday evening, July twenty first I received a letter from Bill saying they were going to be shipped to the Pacific. I thought "Well that probably means I won't be seeing him in the near future; I wonder if I will ever see him again."

July 23rd

I was working evening shift at the factory, when one of the women from Mill bottom came to the machine where I was working, she was so excited, "Kathleen," she said, "your boyfriend is in Mill bottom, asking for you" "I have no boyfriend," I replied. "But he is American and he wants to see you," she replied. He being American I thought I had better check him out. Surprise, there he was. Grinning like a Cheshire cat. I ran to him for a hug and a kiss then went to the foreman to let him know that I was leaving and was not sure when I would be back. I clocked out and we went home.

Bill had been to General Eisenhower's headquarters in order to gain permission to return to England to be married, having told the officer in charge that we'd had all our papers and blood tests and they were all lost in an air raid, they believed him and with permission granted, provided he could find transport, he hitched a ride to England on a transport plane. He had to be back in London the following Tuesday for transport back to Germany, leaving us a very short time to plan a wedding. Ted was now home on furlough, and he had loaned Bill his bicycle, (our only transport other than the bus in war time), a sign that Bill had made a good impression on Ted. My mother and I were not allowed to ride the bike; Ted had it taken it apart when he went into the Army. Little did he know that we put it back together, and before he returned after the war was over, we re-assembled it?

From that time on I always called Ted Pop. On Tuesday Bill and me went to the hospital to see Michael. He was upset. He had always planned on being a pageboy at our wedding. We did our best to console him. He was so little and so cute. It broke my heart to see him so pale and frail. Tuesday afternoon Pop went with us to see the vicar of the Church of England, from there we went to see the Canon. Wednesday we went to York to see the Archbishop of York, to obtain a special license that was needed because the rule of the Churches of England was; as follows 'Before a wedding, Banns must be read during morning worship **three** consecutive Sundays. Otherwise a special license must be obtained from the Archbishop,'

After receiving the license, the Archbishop's secretary invited us to have tea with her, Bill was impressed Leaving York we went back to Hull and went shopping. I bought a wedding dress with borrowed coupons because all clothing was rationed. We bought my bouquet; I wanted a large one as we planned to take it to Raymond's grave after the ceremony. I searched the shops for a decent pair of shoes that were almost impossible to find. I finally found a pair, and was disappointed because there were no white shoes anywhere. In such a short time I had to be satisfied with a light blue waltz length dress, and black shoes. Bill decided we must have some wine, so off we went in search of some, and then back home after such a long day.

We were married on Thursday, July 26[th]1945 at St John the Evangelist Church of England by special license, granted by the Archbishop of York. Bill asked for a glass of wine before we left for the church, I said, "Good Heavens Bill, you can't drink before church," . We had a Rolls Royce Wedding Car thanks to Pop. After the wedding the driver took us to a studio to have our pictures taken, then he drove us home and Bill gave the driver a glass of wine. We had five days together, and then Bill had to return to Germany in order to check back in to Eisenhower's Headquarters, and in November he was discharged from the Army-Air force.

He then began making preparations for my long journey to America. In the meantime, in order to attempt to improve his health, Michael was transferred to a convalescent hospital at Withernsea. (He was still there when I left for America.)

Now that the war was over, the men, coming came back home from the war, were in need of work at the Oil Mill, all female employees were given notice that they were to be terminated in order to make room for the returning men. We were assigned two weeks in order to train the men to take over from us. We did rub it in on them when they had a problem lifting the 100 weight bags. We also enjoyed showing them how we could lift them with no problem. I'm sure they were glad to finally be rid of us.

CHAPTER
6

1946
PREPARING FOR
MY JOURNEY TO AMERICA

Bill's mother and his two sisters Jin, and Kat, often wrote letters to me, Kat would send packages of makeup and other items that we couldn't get in England, she also sent me a lovely two-piece dress. I felt that I had really been accepted into the family, yet even though they seemed anxious to meet me, I couldn't help being concerned about meeting them. Bill was working on the other side of the Atlantic to make preparations for my life in America. He had to have several papers notarized stating that he would be entirely responsible for me, and I would not be a responsibility for The State of Kentucky. He also had to make arrangements with the government for my transportation. I had to obtain a passport, and I also had to have a smallpox vaccination; which made me very ill for two weeks, I felt like I had a really bad case of the flu. I finished my preparations said goodbye to friends and relatives.

The time had finally come for me to leave on the first stage of my journey. It was the second week of April 1946. I had to go to London by train. I said goodbye to Pop, he said, "are you sure you know what you are doing,? you are not going a few miles from home. You are making your bed, and will have to lie in it." I told him I was sure. My mother went to Hull railway station to see me off, she kissed me on my cheek and as we said goodbye, she said, "Take care and write often." I have said before, my mother wasn't one to hug or show a lot of affection. I wondered if she was very sorry to see me go, 'but years later she was to tell me how she felt, and I wished she could have told me there at the station.' The journey traveling alone to London seemed endless, at that time it took almost three hours from Hull.

I finally arrived at Kings Cross Station, there I was met by a bus driver and taken to a bus to wait for other wives to arrive.

When everyone on the bus driver's list was accounted for, he informed us we were ready to leave for Waterloo Train Station. I was so nervous I have no recollection of who met us at the station. I remember being on the train. My nerves had begun to calm down but oh what a long, long, wait on the train that was still in the station. We to begin to move at last, I remember I was getting hungry and I can't remember if we had anything to eat anywhere. Everyone was looking tired and we thought we surely must be near the end of our journey. I was wondering where on earth they were taking us. We learned later that all the waits at each station were for girls coming from different areas of England. I can't remember if there were 200 or 250 of us all of us anxious to see our husbands again.

After what seemed a terribly long time, the train finally came to a stop. We left the train and were transferred to another bus, to be taken at last to our destination. I must say that our journey had been very well organized, but with very little explanation of where we were going. Sighs of relief sounded as we were told that we were almost at the end of our long and tiresome journey where we would stay, until the day we were to sail. We were taken to an American Army Camp in the village of Tidworth, I have no recollection of what time it was when we finally reached our destination.

By this time I was exhausted, I was shown to my quarters, a room with 9 bunk beds, I stepped inside and thought " It looks like I am the only one here." My name was on a top bunk behind the open door. When I looked behind the door, a young girl stood with her head bowed, sobbing and crying, I put my arm around her and asked, "What is your name?" She looked me over and finally dried her eyes and said, "Alma." "What is the matter?" I asked. "I want to go home," she murmured, I did my best to cheer her up. We became good friends; she occupied the bunk below me. German prisoners, who had not yet been released, cleaned our barracks and served our meals. One day we were served wieners, we thought we were being fed raw sausages. The prisoners were very polite, but we avoided them as much as possible. It was hard to forget the years of war and all the air raid bombings. The rest of the girls finally arrived, and claimed the remaining bunks. I made quite a few friends during our stay.

If we went out at night we had to be in by eleven. Of course there had to be one grumpy gal in our midst. I don't remember her name, she wanted to be in bed by nine o'clock and up at six. Time was heavy on our hands so a group of us would go to the village some afternoons to see a movie. It was a very small village. One evening Alma and I decided to make a trip into the village, In case we didn't make it back before curfew, we made arrangements with one of the girls whose bunk was by the window, to make sure it was unlocked, it was low down, and almost reached the floor and easy to open. We were about half an hour late; Alma opened the window and climbed in first, trying to avoid waking anyone who was sleeping. As she stepped inside, she whispered, "Kath, watch your step, there is a coal bucket on the side of the window. Needless to say, clumsy ox that I was, I stepped in the middle of it and woke up the entire room including grumpy. She threatened to report us. Since very one else was laughing, she thought better of it.

We remained at Tidworth for the next few weeks, during which time we had medical exams, more papers to fill out, and money to exchange. Each English pound was worth five American dollars. We were allowed to go to the P.X. where, we could buy snacks and listen to records. Frank Sinatra was a new popular singer in those days and some of the girls were nutty over him. I personally preferred Bing Crosby. We were scheduled to leave about two weeks after we arrived in Tidworth, but we were informed that the ship was in dry dock for repairs, and then some of the crew went on strike for a few days. On May the 16th 1946 we finally received the word that we were scheduled to leave. After more long hours of waiting on busses, finally, we were on our way to South Hampton where we boarded an American Liberty ship. The SS President Tyler, for a 10-day journey across the Atlantic Ocean.

WE SET SAIL

As we left the dock a band was playing Auld Lang Syne. It was a big step that we were taking. I wondered as we sailed further and further from the land where I was born, what was facing me in America. Alma and I were now separated. The ship was very large; I was shown to a 30-bunk cabin below sea level with 29 new bedfellows.

It wasn't too bad I now had new bedmates for 10 days. There was a very large room with showers and toilets. We had the privilege of taking our meals with the officers who were traveling with us; we were fortunate to be sitting at tables, using china dishes with stewards serving us. It really made up for being below sea level. The food was awesome, and there were large bowls of oranges such as we hadn't seen for six years. The remainder of the girls ate with the sailors and crew in the mess hall and was served on trays. We really had the best of it at mealtimes.

The captain sometimes spoke to us over the P.A. "Ladies now hear this there will be a movie showing at such and such a time and place." Or, "there will be entertainment, in a certain place and afterwards refreshments in the mess hall." We, the gals from C deck, after eating in the mess hall, sure did appreciate the Officer's dining rooms. The weather was very balmy and the sailing was quite smooth, except for one day when there were huge swells on the sea, and it became very rough for a little while. Thankfully it didn't last very long. Some of the girls were very seasick. I experienced a few butterflies in my tummy but on the whole I felt fine. About 600 miles from New York the ship broke down. We weren't told what happened but it was finally fixed. And we were on our way again. We thought about the time the ship was in dry dock for repairs, and wondered if we were going to reach New York. There were no more problems; the remainder of the journey was very pleasant. As we sailed into New York on the Hudson River, the captain pointed out The Statue of Liberty, and on the right side the beautiful home of Frank Sinatra. We also noticed a sign on the embankment - FORT HAMILTON was written in huge white letters. Little did we realize some of us would end up in that camp before we reached our final journey.

CHAPTER
7

AMERICA AT LAST

It was late on a Monday afternoon May the 26th 1946 when we finally docked in New York. Another large ship was docked beside us, later we were told that it was a French ship, full of French GI brides. They had already left the ship. After dinner we were told that we would be leaving the next day, we weren't allowed to go ashore; we were to stay in our cabins and wait for further instructions. That evening we were informed that we would be prepared to leave for our final destinations the next morning. At 10 p.m. there was an announcement, "Now hear this. To all Ladies, you are not to leave your cabins until further notice. This is the captain speaking; anyone found on deck will be dealt with immediately." Unfortunately for our group in the lower deck cabin it was most uncomfortable as the air conditioners were out of order.

We finally realized why we were confined to our cabins the crew had all been ashore and returned, to be very blunt they were all drunk and fighting. We could hear cursing and noises that sounded like someone falling. A remark was made from one of the girls, 'what a great introduction to America.' The air conditioner finally came back on and we retired to try and sleep amid all the commotion. The next morning it was a motley crew that were on deck with bruises and black eyes.

Some of the girls left the ship that Tuesday morning, to join their husbands. For some reason a few of us didn't leave that day, I suppose it depended which direction we were headed .We were told that the rest of us we would be leaving the following day. That didn't happen, the trains went on strike at midnight. The girls, who had left, were stranded when the trains stopped. We considered ourselves fortunate to have been left behind. We were shown movies, then taken on a bus tour of New York, much better than staying on the ship trying to keep from being bored. .

On Friday, May 30 the trains were still on strike; Again we were loaded onto buses; another wait (as the army used to say, 'hurry up and wait') We were taken to Fort Hamilton located in Brooklyn; to the Army Camp which we had seen when we sailed up the Hudson River. It was a lovely campsite, quite a change after being on the ocean ten days, staying on the ship anchored in the dock Monday to Friday, except for the short time touring New York City. We were taken to an enormous wooden building with pleasant rooms each with two cots. Shower rooms were down the hall. I had a new roommate. Not far from our building, was a large dining room with more food than we'd seen or tasted during six years of rationing, there was even strawberry shortcake. We were informed that a group of American girls were also staying at the camp; they were on the way to Germany to be with their husbands. They were quarantined because of measles.

My roommate and I became acquainted with one of the American ladies. I can't remember her name; I will call her Mary. She was from Georgia, owned a lovely Buick car, and was allowed to take it with her to Germany. She came to our barracks each morning to take us for a ride. I quickly realized she was quite taken with our accents. Several times after hearing me once she would ask, "Would you please say Kentucky for me again?" The nearest I can write the way I said it was, Kentucky, accent on the Ken. We spent many pleasant hours riding around the camp exchanging interesting stories of our experiences. It was quite a pleasant time at Fort Hamilton accompanied by our lovely chauffeur. The camp was located on a hill; we spent many hours taking in the view of the road below. It was great; we could look down and see the cars on the road below.

We had never seen so many cars as were passing to and fro. Cars in England were kept in the garage for the duration of the war, only farmers, service persons, and busses were allowed petrel. There was a great view of Coney Island Park, and at night after dark, Parachutists could be seen floating down from the sky. The P.X. was stocked with all kinds of goods, stuff that had been rationed to us during the war. While I was browsing around a gentleman, whom I assumed was a reporter, asked me if he could take my picture, I agreed and he proceeded to pick up articles that he assumed would have been rationed; to name a few, a girdle which he suggested I hold it up in front of me, then he picked up a box of soap powder, make up, and other toiletries. Then he thanked me, and said this would be in the Sunday New York Times. I never was able to get a newspaper, but I have often wondered if the article was in the paper, and if so how did it look.

On Monday June 3rd. we were taken for a physical exam, before we could leave for our final journey, it was a real corker of an exam, the doctor asked if we had a sore throat, if we said no, that was it, we were told to carry on. Finally we were leaving; the trains were now running again. We were given name tags and told to wear them at all times. Now I was in Grand Central Train Station waiting for my train, a Pullman Sleeper, another new experience. I was finally on my own, on my way to Ashland Kentucky. I had the top bunk, and didn't sleep much; I was to arrive in Columbus Ohio Tuesday June 4th at eleven a.m. where I had a twelve-hour layover. Then I was to board a train at eleven p.m. for Ashland.

Finally we arrived at Columbus, it was 11 a.m. Tuesday June 4th my luggage was being sent ahead. I put my nametag in my pocket, because I didn't like being stared at or questioned. I was a little nervous as I descended from the train, I was wondering where I should go, when I felt a tap on my shoulder. I was startled and looked around, and to my surprise an Army M.P. was standing there, looking quite annoyed. "Are you Kathleen Price?" He asked, "yes," I said. "Where is your nametag?" He asked." It is in my pocket." I replied. He didn't look very pleased with me, he reminded me that I should be wearing it at all times, until I arrived in Ashland and was met but my husband.

He took me to his office in the Union Station. He was now very pleasant, made sure I had lunch, then accompanied me down the main street and showed me where there was a movie theater and some shops. I went to the movies; I don't remember what was showing. Then I found a shoe shop, I bought a pair of platform heel shoes, and asked the lady clerk if they had any nylons, she very politely informed me that they didn't have any. I went to the cashier, to pay for my shoes, he was a very nice looking friendly gentleman, I thought. "Since he seems much friendlier than the clerk, I will ask him also." I said, "excuse me, do you have any nylons?" I guess he recognized my British accent, because he asked if I was one of the war brides from England. I told him I was, and that I was on my way to Ashland Kentucky to join my husband. He said, "I think I can find you a pair," then he went into the back room, and came out with my first ever pair of nylons.

Finally it was 11 p.m. I boarded the train for my final destination. I was really beginning to feel anxious: Would I remember what Bill looked like since it had been 11 months since I last saw him? Would his family like me? The closer we came to Ashland the more nervous I became. It was about 1 a.m. Wednesday morning June 5th. When I finally arrived in Ashland Ky. I became more reassured as Bill, his sister Jin, her husband Herstle and Herb Jr. (Bill's brother Herb's son.) met me with hugs by everyone, telling me how good it was that I was there at last. I must say the American army certainly should have been commended for doing an awesome job of taking care of all of us apart from the hours of waiting it was a great journey. I could now relate to the army and all the service persons for their comments "it is always hurry up and wait"

And so began my life in the United States of America: I can't begin to tell how strange I felt in this new country.

\\

LIFE IN ASHLAND KY
THE FIRST 7 YEARS

I was relieved to finally be settled in my new home after traveling so long. Bill and I began our life together in a small apartment in the lower level of Jin and Herstle's home. I must say my welcome was over whelming, as I don't ever remember being hugged by anyone in England. We were a very reserved people. I met my mother in law and father in law John and Viola Price, they were much older than my parents, I later referred to them as Granny and Poppaw (popular KY name for grandpa). Bill had two brothers Herb and wife Mary; (Herb was always known as Peg, the result of holding a stick of dynamite that blew off his finger) name stuck to him the rest of his life. Next Robert, (Bob) wife Alice, three sisters, Virginia, (Jin) Husband, Herstle, Katherine, (Kat) husband Red, and Margarite (Mag.) There were numerous aunts, uncles, nieces, nephews, and cousins. Eventually I met them all.

I was very shy and the culture shock was a little overwhelming; me with my Yorkshire accent and all the strange foods such as pinto beans, corn bread, sweet potatoes, and many more. Biscuits in England are cookies in America. Sweets in America are candies. The pronunciations for instance, tomatoes instead of my Tomatoes. One day I asked the clerk in a store for some aspirins (aspirins) and she asked, "What flavor do you want?" Oh" I asked, "do they come in flavors?" "Vanilla, chocolate and strawberry," she replied. She thought I had asked for ice cream. We visited relatives quite frequently, and being shy and very much aware of my accent, I always begged Bill, "please, don't go off with the men and leave me with the women." "Oh I won't," he would answer, but before many minutes passed he was gone, and there I was left feeling mortified; mostly I would just sit and listen, feeling awkward among so many strangers. I finally overcame some of my shyness as I became more and more acquainted with everyone.

For about three months all went very well, until one day Bill came in from work in a bad humor, His clothes were wet, he had been caught in a rainstorm, he sat around in his wet clothes and I told him he should change into some dry clothes. He became angry with me and said I was not to give him orders and he walked out, wet clothes and all. He was gone for hours and when he came back he was staggering, very drunk. That was the beginning of seven years during which, many were the times when I wished I were back in England. My mother in law and I became very close; from here on I shall refer to her as Granny Price. Jin told me that my mother had written and asked if she would take her place. Jin certainly was a second mother to me. I would never have made it without her and Granny. There were good times between Bill's episodes of drinking. It became obvious that he was an alcoholic. His sister Mag was also an alcoholic and they would drink together. Ashland was dry; no alcohol was allowed to be sold they had to go to Ironton Ohio to buy beer. There were places in Ashland where alcohol was sold illegally, and of course Bill new all of them.

I became pregnant with our first child; I was very ill with morning sickness that lasted most of the nine months. I was very ignorant and asked Jin lots of questions since back in my youth mothers didn't tell daughters much about facts of life. Around my fourth month Granny called Jin and asked if I had felt life yet. Jin laughed and said, "She is so ignorant, she wouldn't know if she had," then made sure I knew she was joking. I let it be known that if we had a girl she must be named Sheila, in memory of my best childhood friend Sheila.

I always looked forward to letters from home; mother would keep me informed about Michael who was still in the convalescent hospital in Withernsea; a seaside town. In one of the letters I received, mother wrote that when she had visited him he asked, "mummy, was Jesus shot?" she thought that was a strange question and replied, "No Michael, he was hanged on a cross, why do you ask?" "Well," he said, "when I say my prayers I always say; 'Our Father what shot in Heaven." Mother said he was always talking about God and one day he asked if Jesus could bake, she said she asked why he wanted to know. His reply was "Well today is Poggy's birthday and I wondered if Jesus would bake a cake for him."

1947 - 1949

April 12th

Our first child was born Our lovely little girl was finally here. I told Bill I would like to name her Sheila Kay In memory of my best childhood friend. I made a vow to myself that I would never, ever leave my child or any future children that I may have, no matter what the circumstances became. I wrote and let mother know she was a grandma. She wrote back and said how thrilled she was but at the same time sad, as this was her first grandchild and she couldn't get to see her. When Sheila was 2 months old I received word that Michael had died. That was a sad day for me being so far away. A terrible time for Mother, that was two boys now in heaven, and was left with only one boy my brother Jimmy now eleven years old, Teddy, who lived with his dad, would now be seventeen in November, we had no idea where he was, and I was three thousand miles away in America. Was it any wonder that some years later she ended up in the hospital with a nervous breakdown? She sent a package for Sheila at least once a month, she kept her clothed, and loaded her with toys.

Life went on, with Bill drinking more, and more, and we decided it was time to move to a place of our own. We found a double that looked clean, and we met our new neighbors Ruby and Everett with whom we became great friends. We finally moved in, Sheila was 10 months old. That night we put Sheila in her crib, turned the lights out and got in bed. I had asked Bill to turn the lights on for some reason and HORRORS! An army of cockroaches came out; I was terrified, never had I seen anything like them. We got spray and tried to get rid of them, but the final straw was when one got in Bill's ear. We packed our clothes and Sheila's crib, the rest of the stuff belonged in the apartment. We made sure that none of those horrors traveled with us and moved in with Granny and Papaw. We stayed there till we found another place .

WE BOUGHT OUR FIRST HOUSE

Everett phoned Bill to say that his uncle had two houses for sale and asked if we would be interested in buying one for $2500.00. Three rooms and bath, can you imagine we could get a house for that price back in those days? We got it for no down payment and twenty- five dollars a month mortgage. It needed a little work done, but Bill worked on fixing the needed repairs. We had to buy few needed pieces of furniture, and moved in. Sheila was almost a year old. Once again we were neighbors with Ruby and Everett. As we settled in our new home I wondered where my old friend Sue was living, I knew Cecil was from Iowa, so I wrote a letter to Mrs. Wilson, Sue's mother in England, and asked if she would please mail Sue's address to me. I received a letter back from Mrs. Wilson with Sue's address and phone number in Waterloo Iowa. I phoned Sue and we made plans to visit her and Cecil in the summer of 1949 when Sheila was 2 yrs old.

We began our journey leaving Ashland one day in the early morning. We drove until late afternoon and decided to stop in Dayton, Ohio where we found a hotel to stay overnight. After we ate dinner, Bill decided he needed to go out for cigarettes, he said he wouldn't be gone long, I knew better. Time passed and he didn't return so I waited about two hours and said to Sheila, "let's go find daddy." I had an idea where I would find him. At the first bar we came to we stopped and I peered inside the door; I didn't want to go all the way in with Sheila. Sure enough there he was, sitting at the bar drinking beer. He caught sight of us, and rose out of his seat, took Sheila by the hand and began showing her around. She thought it was great. I finally got him to leave. We arrived back at the hotel and I put Sheila to bed then I gave Bill a piece of my mind. I was furious.

We resumed our journey the next morning and drove as far as Kokamo, Indiana. There was a heavy storm, lots of lightning and thunder, so we decided to stop at a hotel. When we left the next morning we were glad we had stayed; it had been a terrible storm. As we traveled a few miles we realized, if we hadn't stopped we would have been caught in the middle of the storm. We saw quite a lot of damage the storm had caused. Our first stop after filling the car with gas was to buy some of his favorite beverage; he bought 12 bottles of beer. I kept begging him not to drink so much. By the time we reached Waterloo it was late very dark, there was no GPS in those days to guide us to the address. It was difficult to see the numbers on the houses and to coin an old phrase Bill was feeling his cheerios. He had managed to drink all twelve beers on the way. We finally found the house.

I roused Sheila from her sleep. Cecil and Sue were waiting for us, with all the lights on inside and outside to guide us, it was great seeing them again. We stayed almost a week and I was embarrassed by Bill's actions. Sue begged me to stay with them, "no," I replied, I made my bed I shall lie in it." I thought of those words Pop had said. As we said our goodbyes, we invited Sue and Cecil to be sure and come to Ohio for a visit, and went on our way.

Home again, due to illness, Bill's dad had to retire from his work at the golf course. The owner liked Bill and hired him take over as supervisor in place of his dad. Bill was doing better, not drinking so much, till one day his boss sent him to town for supplies. He returned to work late in the afternoon, staggering drunk and causing a scene. He was locked in the building that housed the lawn mowers and tractors, because he always had keys with him for tractors he had the means to start one, which he did, and drove it through the locked door. Needless to say he lost his supervisor position and went back to mowing again. Most weekends when he came home in bad shape I would take Sheila and go to Jin and Herstle's and stay there till he sobered up.

November 1949 I was very ill, and in a lot of pain. I was admitted to the hospital where I had a partial hysterectomy, one tube, and one ovary removed. One Saturday a few days after I had my stitches removed Herb; Bill's oldest brother (as *previously mentioned known as Peg*) called and asked Bill to meet him at his house in Westwood, a suburb of Ashland. Then he wanted Bill to go with him to the home of Mary's parents in Flatwoods to help kill and dress a pig. Sheila and I went with him as far as Peg and Mary's house and we stayed there. Sheila was happy because her Aunt Jin and uncle Herstle lived next door and she could run over there and visit. Television had just come to our area and our nephew Herb Jr. who was two years younger than me, and was my very good friend, had bought the first television sold in Westwood. Herb Jr. was pretty popular with his friends who were all anxious to visit in order check it out. I was still not feeling well after my surgery so Mary suggested I rest on their bed; I was glad to lie there for a while.

Later she turned the television on; there was only one station. I was watching the Christmas movie, Scrooge, when Peg and Bill returned. Both of them were very drunk. Bill came in the bedroom and said, "let's go. " "Can't you wait until I finish watching this movie?" I asked. I would rather have waited a while for him to sober up .He pulled my arm and he said, "I said let's go," with that, Peg got hold of Bill and said "Don't you touch her." "She is my wife and I'll touch her if I want," replied Bill and the fight began; they fought all over the living room and broke a lamp. Bill got the worst of it; a cut on his forehead, and his top lip was split. I was glad Sheila had gone over to Jin and Herstle's. Mary got Peg settled down and saw to his wounds. I was so embarrassed.

I apologized to Mary. I went over to Jin and Herstle's to pick up Sheila. I asked Herstle if he would help me get Bill in the car and then drive us home because I didn't drive. He agreed and we finally got Bill home I went next door to Everett and Ruby's house and asked if Everett would help get Bill in the house. Everett and Herstle got him inside. Everett cleaned the cut over Bill's lip, pulled together the cut on his forehead, and cleaned and placed a band-aid on it. I thanked Herstle and Everett and asked Herstle to take the car to his house, and when Bill was sober, he could take the bus to pick up the car..

Herstle left and I put Sheila to bed and finally got Bill settled and in bed. All night long he would jump up in bed and yell, "where's my shot gun I'm going to shoot Peg." *(Now, I don't like guns and have never had one or used one. At that time I felt like I could have used one on Bill)* He was one sorry person the next morning. He vowed he would stop drinking. For a few weeks he did quite well and I thought maybe he meant it, but then he had a brainwave. He would make his own beer. He purchased a five-gallon crock, plus the necessary ingredients proceeded to make home brew in the bathroom. He washed his bottles in the bathtub. When the brew had done whatever it had to do, he would take a cipher hose and siphon the beer from the crock into the bottles. He would suck on the hose to start the beer running into the bottles and by the time he had them all filled you can imagine the state he was

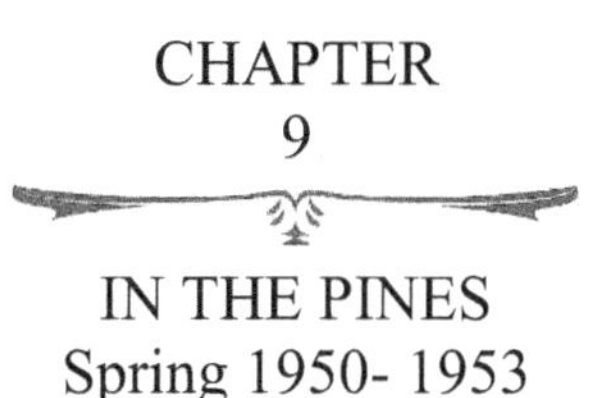

CHAPTER
9

IN THE PINES
Spring 1950- 1953

We sold our house, and began looking for a rental; I really don't know why we sold the house. We didn't find a rental right away so we moved in with Bill's cousin Lawrence and wife Joann. Bill and Lawrence both drank a lot so that episode didn't last long. We finally found a place in Bellefonte. It belonged to one of the top car salesmen in Ashland, it was a block building with kitchen, living area, two bedrooms and large bathroom; It had been built for the purpose of raising chickens. Instead it was used by the owner to live in until the completion of the new home he was having built; thus he decided to rent it. The house wasn't much but I loved the surroundings, pine trees, and lots of green grass. In summer huge, delicious dewberries grew under the pine trees. It was a great place for Sheila, especially when Ruby and Everett visited with their two boys David and Cecil.

About that time the house in Bellefonte where Granny and Poppaw lived, had to be vacated. A land developer had bought the area, and the old houses were to be torn down, because new homes were to be built replacing the old ones. Granny and Poppaw moved in with us in the pines. Sheila was a happy camper. Every morning her Poppaw would take her for a walk up a nearby hillside. She still talks about it; she was about 3 years old when we moved there. He showed her how he could make the eagle on a silver dollar cry. She spent hours with a dollar coin trying to make it cry, and would come to her daddy and me and ask, "Why can't I make it cry like Poppaw?" He also taught her something called mumble pegs. I taught her lots of little songs and stories from my childhood. One story about a pig that wouldn't cross over a bridge, it was her favorite story, and she demanded that Poppaw tell it to her. He explained that he couldn't tell the story to her because he didn't know the story. She was so upset, I finally wrote it down for him so that he could read the story to her, which he did, and once again she was happy.

Bill was now close to his work at the Bellefonte Golf Club, when one day he had a flat tire, and he had to walk to work. Later that day, I decided that I could change the flat tire, I jacked the car up, removed the wheel with the flat tire, then I removed the spare wheel from the trunk, and placed it on the car. I was so proud of myself, and when it was time for Bill to quit work, I told Sheila, "Let's take the car, and go pick up daddy." It was the first and last time I ever drove a car with a stick shift. Bill was pleasantly surprised, and bragged to the guys about having a clever wife. As we left the Golf Course driveway and drove onto the road I looked at him and said, "How long are you going to drive on the wrong side of the road?" He gave me a hard look and Sheila said, "she wouldn't listen daddy, she just wouldn't listen, I tried to tell her she was driving on the wrong side of the road; I was so embarrassed. Later Bill's sister-in-law Mary told us that she and her sister Pauline were driving by the golf course as I on the way to get Bill. She said she made the statement, "Oh look, Pauline, they must have a new mailman in Bellefonte. Oh my goodness it is Kathleen and she is driving on the wrong side of the road." Needless to say I lost my nerve and didn't learn to drive until much later in life.

Ruby and Everett and their two boys, David and Cecil, would visit us quite often. The boys always enjoyed visiting with Sheila. We lived there for about two years. During the winter months while the golf course was closed, Bill was able to stay employed by working on the tractors and equipment. We finally decided to move, as the house was really damp in winter. Sheila was very frail and easily came down with bronchitis.

We moved down the road to Hoods Creek Pike. We had moved so many times that I look back and wonder how we ever made it. I wrote many letters home but I would remember the words my stepfather said as I was leaving. "You are not going only a few miles from home. You have made your bed and you will have to lie in it." The letters always ended being torn up. Actually, Sheila was the main reason for keeping me in America. I had vowed that I would never leave a child of mine no matter what the cost. Sheila was an American citizen I was still a British subject. I knew that Granny, Poppaw, Jin, and Herstle would fight to keep her; she was the apple of their eyes.

I have hated telling about this phase of our lives I am not going to go into all of it. I feel that this had to be told in order to see what an amazing change the next years brought to our lives. It has shown me that through all this misery; God had a plan for our lives. Another new experience awaited me, entering Sheila into first grade at School. The school system was quite different from our British schools. Fortunately Sheila enjoyed school, Bill's fifteen year old niece, Billie Jean was living with us and was a great babysitter for Sheila.

GOD HAS A WAY OF GETTING OUR ATTENTION!

FEBRUARY 1953

Little by little I began to pay attention to God. I always prayed, but never really believed that I was important enough for God to pay attention to me, yet I always felt that He protected us during the war. I began working at a drive in restaurant, The Big Mug. (Owned by B.E.Gibbs. Manager Phil Quant.) My salary was 50 cents an hour plus uniforms. It was now around February 1953 I was working every day. After school, Billie Jean was baby-sitting with Sheila. Every Saturday night I was required to close the restaurant, empty the cash register, count the money, and take it home with me. Phil partied on Saturday nights and left me in charge. On Sunday mornings I had to open the restaurant because Phil attended church. He told me one day that he felt guilty keeping me from church on Sundays, I told him not to worry, as I didn't go to church anyway. He must have been a little worried about his drinking on Saturdays, and Church on Sunday as he went on to tell me that his minister preached "Don't do as I do, do as I say"

Quite often I began thinking about going to church. Bill's brother Bob and wife Alice were devout Christians and attended church every Sunday. One day as I was busy waiting on a customer, a gentleman entered the restaurant he sat at the counter and ordered a hamburger and coffee. There was something strange about him that bothered me. I was smoking a cigarette at the time and for some reason, I hid it behind me. He didn't say much, just looked at me with a kind look. When I returned home I told Bill about this man who came in the restaurant and looked at me very strangely, but kindly. Bill made light of it and said he was probably flirting with me. I disagreed with him, because it was nothing like that. The next time the man came in the restaurant, I asked, "Who are you?" He said, "My name is Bill Doughty and I am a preacher." That stunned me, he didn't look like my idea of what a preacher should looked like; He said he had a radio program every Saturday morning, mentioned the station he was on and invited me to listen, I never did.

The next day two men came in the restaurant and began talking about church services they had been attending. I began to look forward to the times when they came at lunchtime, and enjoyed waiting on them; they introduced themselves, one was Johnny Green. The other was Elwood Gibbs son of B.E. Gibbs the owner of the restaurant. They were very friendly and I listened to their conversations about how they had recently been attending church services. Johnny always called me Sunshine. This was all new to me, I really was interested, but there was so much I didn't understand. (I look back now as I write and I can see how God was slowly sending in these people to the restaurant. All three of them became very much a part of our lives,)

Now God was really working on me. Our previous neighbors Everett and Ruby began visiting us every Saturday, asking us to go to Church with them the next evening. They were attending a revival that was being held in the Baptist church at Worthington Ky. I really wanted to go to church, but Bill would not be persuaded, and I didn't want to go without him. I had no idea what a revival consisted of. I was most miserable and I had trouble sleeping. Around midnight, as a train went through Ashland, the engineer would blow a very loud horn. The first time it woke me I jumped up in bed scared out of my wits. I thought it was Gabriel blowing his trumpet bringing Jesus to end the world. Bill woke up and wanted to know what on earth was wrong. I tried to make light of it, and told him I thought I had heard a noise and told him to go back to sleep.

One Saturday when Ruby and Everett visited, I promised to go to church with them the following Sunday evening, but by Friday I lost my nerve. I talked Bill into taking me to West Virginia to visit his sister Kat and husband Red McNeil. We got Sheila ready, and a grouchy husband complained most of the way there. I just couldn't face Ruby and Everett after making a promise to them. I am thankful that they didn't lose heart; they still kept coming. On the sixth Saturday, I promised I would go to the revival with them the next evening.

MARCH 8 1953

That was a Sunday I shall never forget. In the afternoon as I was washing the dinner dishes, (my sink was in front of a window that overlooked a creek in the back of our home.) I couldn't keep my mind off the fact that Ruby and Everett would be there to ask us to go to church with them for the six o'clock service. I thought, 'I really will go tonight,' then I would think, 'No I won't go' I struggled with thoughts of what would it be like, would I understand any of it? Finally I just determined that I was going. I asked Bill if he would go, he said, "No, I will stay home and take care of Sheila, you can go without me." I figured I had better wear a hat. I should definitely not go to church without a hat. When Ruby and Everett arrived I was dressed in my Sunday best. As we walked in the church I looked around, it looked pretty much like an English Wesleyan chapel; nothing like the Church of England and none of the women wore hats.

I was a bit shocked seeing the Evangelist, because he was dressed in a regular suit and not a robe. I can't remember what his message was about, but I did enjoy the hymns, because some of them were familiar to me, we used to sing them during school assembly. At the end of the service, the minister asked if anyone would like to come forward to accept Christ as Savior. I can't begin to describe how I felt, I wanted to go forward, but I had no idea what to do if I did go. As I was standing by my seat, a small voice in my mind said, 'Kathleen walk down the aisle.' I stood there shaking, as they sang Pass me not oh Gentle Savior, I finally walked down the aisle, no one else went down. I stood there and thought 'now what?' Again the voice spoke in my mind, "now kneel." And so I knelt and all I knew to say was "God forgive me." I *rose* to my feet believing with all my heart that God had heard and forgiven me.

Never in all my life had I felt such peace. People began to crowd around me, the men shaking my hand, the women hugging me. In an instant my life was changed and later I learned as I read my bible that I had experienced what Jesus meant when He said Ye must be born again, I had never seen anyone go to an altar to be saved but that night I experienced it. I don't know who my earthly father is, but now I am a child of the King, God is my Father and Jesus is my Brother. When Everett and Ruby let me off at home the house was all in darkness so they didn't stop by. I went in and Bill and Sheila were in bed. Bill had been listening for the car to bring me home and he had jumped in bed with his clothes on. I went into the bedroom and turned on a night-light. He looked up rubbing his eyes pretending to be sleepy. He took one look at me and jumped up and said, "You Got Saved." He later told me my face had a glow on it.

Keep in mind this was the sixth week that this revival has been going on. Usually the longest they went was two weeks, no longer than three weeks and seldom that long. The next night I was ready when Ruby and Everett came to pick me up, again Bill wouldn't go. That night when I arrived home he was in bed again, I didn't turn on a light, I could see from the light in the living room, I just walked up to the bed. I knew he was awake and I whispered in his ear, " I prayed for you tonight." He began crying and sobbing, he got out of bed and knelt down and began to pray. He got up and said, "It's no use. I guess I have to go to church." He later told that he had made his brags that he would never go to an altar in front of everyone. So I guess he had to show God that he didn't mean it.

On Tuesday March 10th Bill came in from work and changed clothes and we got Sheila ready and went to Ruby and Everett's house, They were just eating dinner, "Where are you going Bill?" Everett asked. "To church," said Bill. Everett got all excited and said, "Well Praise the Lord" and missed the table as he slapped his hand down and it landed in his plate. What a time those two had, rejoicing and hugging each other. That night Bill settled it all with God and from that night till the day he died he never touched another drop of alcohol. When we arrived home after church, it was a different Bill Price, he said, "I have to call mom and tell her the news." What a time of rejoicing, even though granny hadn't been attending church she was thrilled with the news.

I had yet another new experience ahead of me. The following Sunday afternoon we were to be baptized.

I had never even heard of a Baptizing only sprinkling. I always worried because we never had Sheila Christened. Whenever I mentioned it to Bill, he would tell me not to worry as we don't Christen babies here as they do in England. We went to church the remainder of the week and enjoyed the services. The revival closed with the Baptizing, which was held in the very creek that ran behind our house. There was a place just down the road from where we lived called Hoods Creek Falls, it was an ideal place the rocks formed a falls it was a lovely place. There was a large sandy area beside the creek where people could gather.

Bill had explained to me how a baptizing was performed. I told him that I thought we should hang back so I could see how it was done. I don't swim and I was a little concerned. There were two or three more couples that were to be baptized. I looked around and I couldn't believe the crowd that was gathering there. It was a beautiful sunshiny day and it looked like everyone who knew Bill Price, had come to see him be baptized; the news had got around already. The closer it came time for the service to begin Bill and I had moved up to the water's edge and the minister took us in first. Again I experienced something I had never seen before. I now realize that God kept that revival going for six weeks, for Bill and me.

OUR NEW LIVES BEGINS

I wrote to mother and told her that God had forgiven me; I had been saved, and was now a Christian. She wrote back and said, "why do you need to be saved and forgiven, you haven't been bad." I had to write and tell her that she didn't know all that I had done. I suppose she felt the same way I did when I first came to America. I didn't understand how people could talk so freely about God, the Bible, and Jesus. I was very confused until gradually, I began to have a desire to attend church. I have come to realize that God must have been instrumental in deciding where in America would be the best place for me. Kentucky is a part of the south, known as the Bible-Belt. (*It now seemed even more evident to me, that God had been listening to my prayers, asking Him to please don't let me die, keeping in mind that on that fateful night, when we met Bill and Cecil, they were the only G.I.'s who visited the Six Bells in July 1944,and it was Saturday night, when usually there would be a large number*)

We attended the church in Wurtland for a few Sundays, but decided we should find a church closer to home. We surprised Bob and Alice by attending 21st ST Tabernacle where they were members; they were so pleased and introduced us to the pastor E.A Curry, who became a great help to me, taking me under his wing so to speak. He always referred to me as his little English girl. Lo and behold who do you think was a member of that church? Sure enough it was Johnny Green. What a time this was as I grew in knowledge of God's way of Life. Bill was a changed man, no more beer, no more using bad language by either of us. What a difference it made in our lives. I didn't have to worry about him coming home drunk. Sheila was happy to have daddy taking us to church and spending so much more time with her.

Several weeks passed, Ruby and Everett had found a small church. Located not very far from our home The FAIRVIEW MISSION.

One Sunday morning we decided to visit the church. As we walked in the Pastor greeted us, shook my hand, and said, "My children's Sunday School teacher wasn't able to be here today, would you please be willing to take her place?" I was dumb founded I had never taught a class in my life. I said I'm sorry I have no idea how to teach a class." He wouldn't take no for an answer, he said he felt very impressed to ask. I thought about the times when as a child I always wanted to go to the chapel when a certain minister was the speaker, because somewhere in his message he had a story for the children. Believe it or not I said I would give it a try. I taught the class, and that was the beginning of my interest in Child Evangelism.

We attended the mission for quite some time and became friends with the pastor, Rev. Charles Sands, and his wife Evelyn. I continued to teach the children every Sunday. In the meantime, Bill Doughty my preacher from the Big Mug was preaching in a revival at Summit Ky. Nazarene church, we decided to attend one evening, at the close of the service we had a chat with Bill, and he asked if we would do someone a favor. Two ladies who had arrived in a taxi, and needed a ride home; the two ladies were Mondane Horne, and her sister Wilma Fields. It was no trouble taking them home because they lived only a short distance from our home. From that introduction, Mondane and I became close friends, and an important part of our lives.

Bill only had an eighth grade education, he only attended high school for a few weeks, because he had to walk or ride his bike to school, and it was quite a long way to Russell KY. He quit school and went to work at a service station. (*A place where he often had access to the beer he once loved.*) Now, no more did I have to worry when he went to work at the golf course, he always came straight home after work, and was always sober. What a joy it was, but I had a problem. I was having a hard time trying to quit smoking; I was really trying. One evening Sheila came to me, crying, "mommy I can't see." It was as if an onionskin covered her eyes; it was so strange.

We knew we would have to take her to the doctor the next day. I was so worried, and my voice in my mind again spoke to me and said, "What means the most to you your cigarettes or your child's eyes, I immediately prayed, and promised God I would never again touch another cigarette, but would He please heal Sheila's eyes. The next morning the first thing she did when she awoke was to run to her daddy, crying, "Daddy, daddy, my eyes are better;" this was my **first miracle**. I realized that even though our lives had changed we were not perfect. I have never touched another cigarette, and I didn't even want one anymore, a short time after, Bill was also able to quit smoking

We continued attending services at Fairview, studying God's word, and growing in knowledge of the Christian faith. One night I had a strange dream, I dreamed that Bill was telling me that he felt God was calling him to the ministry. I told Billie Jean the words that I dreamed Bill had told to me. I asked her to not say anything to anyone but keep it in mind; and be sure not to say anything to Bill. A few weeks passed, and I hadn't thought anymore about the dream. Then one Sunday night, as we were driving home from church, Bill said, "I have something to tell you" "oh what is it?" I asked. He began to tell us that he felt God was calling him to the ministry. He repeated the exact words that I had told Billie Jean from my dream. "Oh aunt Kathleen" she said loudly in my ear, "it is just like you said in your dream." That was a time of rejoicing. Of course we had to tell Everett and Ruby, they were so happy to hear it.

A few weeks later around the last week in October 1953, Ruby approached Bill and asked if he would go to Oil Springs, Ky where her parents and bother lived. There weren't any churches in that area. There was a small building a few yards from her parents' home that was once a schoolhouse and was empty. Her brother had access to the key. She said she had been thinking about how it would be good to open that schoolhouse and have Bill preach his first sermon and have a weekend revival. She said she couldn't get it off her mind, we prayed about it, and felt it was God's Will that we should go.

We began making plans to go, Bill was very nervous; he spent much time studying and praying. Ruby contacted her brother and parents and we set off in early November Bill, Sheila, and me, in our car, and Ruby and Everett in theirs. Billie Jean had decided to visit her mother, (Bill's sister Mag) while we were gone. It had been snowing, the roads were now clear.

However, we were in for a real surprise, the final road to Ruby's parents' home was very narrow and muddy, we stopped and had a short conference on whether to go on or turn back, we finally decided that if this was God's will He would help us get there, so we set off again and made it safely without any problems.

Ruby's brother and some neighbors had taken extension cords from his house to the school house, there was a heater in the building, in which they built a fire, and with extension cords and lamps we were able to have light, and the building was ready for our use. We were served a dinner on arrival, and then prepared for the service. I don't remember the text Bill used, but that was his first message, and the results of that service were awesome. As the service came to a close, a man approached Bill and Everett, and told them that he had spent years in prison, for killing someone. He said that he was told that God would have nothing to do with him and there was no hope for him to be forgiven. Bill quoted scriptures to him and told him of God's Grace, and how Jesus died for even the chiefs' of sinners, the man was sobbing with grief; he fell on his knees and asked for God's forgiveness, he accepted Christ into his heart and there was great rejoicing that night, others came to the Lord including Ruby's brother.

We stayed with Ruby's brother and family, as bedtime came the fire was built up to stay warm during the night, it was cold in our bedroom. Sheila slept in the middle between Bill and me, I was very thin, because my health was poor at the time, and there were so many quilts on the bed, that every time I wanted to turn over I had to ask Bill to raise the covers so that I could turn. We didn't get much sleep trying to keep Sheila warm. Morning finally dawned and we made our way to the kitchen, where we joined Ruby's family. A delicious country breakfast had been prepared for us. With our stomachs full we prepared for the long journey home. As we were saying our goodbyes, everyone was rejoicing, and telling how they had enjoyed the service. I must say that I was amazed at the waybill, with no high school education, and no seminary attendance was able to understand God's work, preach an amazing message and deal with a grief stricken man with such positive results. I realized it came from much prayer and study of God's word. A few years later we were told that the same man who was converted that night, had helped build a large church in that area and was doing a great work in leading others to Christ.

At the Fairview mission, Mondane and I began singing together during services, Modane played the piano, I sang soprano, and Dane as we called her sang alto. Sheila was always saying she wished she had a sister. One day we found her on her knees beside her bed, praying that God would make her doll come alive, because she wanted a sister. Mother was very interested in my letters about our new lives. One day we heard about a man who owned a machine that made records, and was available for a price, to take his machine to a customer's home, and make a record. We contacted him, and arranged to have him come to our home, and make a record. Mondane and I sang the. Gospel song 'My Sins Are Gone' these are the words of the first verse.

You ask me why I'm happy, so I'll just tell you why
Because, my sins are gone, and when I meet the scoffers
Who ask me where they are I say, my sins are gone
They're underneath the blood on the cross of Calvary
As far removed from darkness is from dawn
In the sea of God's forgetfulness,
That's good enough for me Praise God my sins are gone

It was quite exciting to hear our voices recorded, and it sounded great, and had turned out very well. I mailed it to mother, she wrote back and said how she enjoyed it; the words she wrote "you really are happy now aren't you." A short time later, I received a letter from her telling how she couldn't stop grieving over losing Michael and Raymond, she had been to see the doctor and she said he told her he couldn't help her any more, she needed to help herself. Ted told her they were his boys too, and asked, what would happen if he gave up. She said that for the first time since she was sixteen she prayed, and it was as if a light broken through; she remembered the words from a song that was in a hymn book which I had sent to her; the title of it was 'God is gathering little bulbs for His garden,' she said her little buds were now in His Garden and someday she would see them again. I did thank God for that letter; I had been worried about mother, she had lost two boys in death and one left behind and I was three thousand miles away. After this her letters were much more cheerful.

1955 -1959

SHEILA LOSES HER BEST FRIEND

JUNE 1955 was a sad month Papaw was very ill, Bill and I stood by his bed as he breathed his last breath, as granny was taking care of Sheila, knowing this was going to be a difficult, telling her that the grandpa she loved so well, had gone to be with Jesus. As young as she was she still remembers all the good times they had together, and talks of them often. Many friends attended his funeral; He was well known and respected. Sheila and granny became closer. It was about this time that Herstle found two baby ground hogs on the railroad, a train had killed the mother. He brought these cute little babies to Sheila, just the right time to take her mind off her papaw.

She named them Suzy and Jerry. They were very clean and used a box of soil to do their business. There were no litter boxes back then. Sometimes she would take them to bed with her, granny didn't approve of them. She would check to see if they were in bed with Sheila, when Sheila heard granny approaching ,she would hide Suzy and Jerry in her pajamas. It was surprising how she kept them quiet. They were funny and so tame, Sheila would give them an ice cream cone, and they would take it in their front paws, turning it round and round as they ate. I shall always have a soft place for ground hogs. (*I must add this information,*)---Usually in summer, Sheila and I always check the roadside for ground hogs, they can usually be seen munching the grass. We always have a good laugh talking about how people would think we were crazy, watching for ground hogs. We are always disappointed when there aren't any, we have a lot of laughs over them. We still think they are cute, and we will always remember Suzy and Jerry.

OUR FIRST PASTORATE

Elwood was the Pastor of the Boyd County Tabernacle located a few miles west of Ashland. We began visiting services there. In the fall of 1955, Elwood felt that his it was time for him to move on, He wanted to form a Rescue Mission; Elwood's father helped him organize The Rescue Mission church on Route sixty in Ashland. Bill was asked to meet with the board members of the Tabernacle, for permission to take Elwood's place as their pastor. The results were a vote of 100% to accept him, we made many new friends during that term. While we were there, Sheila got her wish, her baby sister was born, of course she asked if she could name her, thus Nov. 20th 1956 Katherine Ann was born. She was a lovely baby; her name became shortened to Kathy. She had a tendency to become car sick if we had to drive very long distances. She was a very good baby; Sheila would take care of her during the services.

Bill became very well known in many different churches. Mondane and I sang during the services. I had always had a desire to sing and now God was making it possible. My voice was becoming quite good, when I was alone I would exercise my voice until I could reach high c then finally high e and was able to sing the song I loved, I'm going higher someday. We remained at the tabernacle until Kathy was 10 months old. The Rescue Mission was now growing; with a large congregation Elwood approached Bill, asking if he would consider joining him as his associate. Bill told him he would have to pray about it, and he had to bring it before the board members of the tabernacle, he struggled with the decision and much prayer. He finally felt it was God's Will to make the change. The congregation at the tabernacle was very sad to see us go. We stayed until a new pastor was installed.

Thus began our affiliation with God's Rescue Mission, we became close friends with Betty and Walter Stone. This was a much larger church, being an associate pastor 'Bill was able to accept requests from other churches to hold a revival, and I had to rely on Walter and Betty to take the children and me to church on the Sundays when Bill would be gone in a revival. I still hadn't got up nerve to drive the car. It was good that the bus went past our house several times on weekdays. Every morning at ten a.m. we broadcast the RESCUE HOUR direct from the church to the radio station, On Sundays, after Morning Worship we traveled to the TV station at Huntington West Virginia where we began to broadcast the RESCUE HOUR, which grew to a large viewing audience of four thousand listeners, and a large mailing list of close to two thousand. Bill and Mondane worked in the office in Ashland Ky, and published a monthly mailing magazine.

Bill became Pastor of The Rescue Mission, while in the meantime; Elwood bought a very large tent that seated 500 people. The Rescue Hour became well known in what was called the Tri State of Ky, W.VA, and Ohio. Mondane, Elwood's sister, Dorla, and I became the RESCUE HOUR TRIO. Kathy no longer sat quietly in the church; she became quite popular with the teenage girls as she was passed from one to another.

On May 16th 1958 our oldest boy was born, we named him William Michael after his daddy and my brother Michael. Life was great now; Bill was so proud of our son, he said, "he thought every man should have a son." We continued to pastor the Rescue Mission and take care of the morning broadcasts, and Sunday television programs. Elwood was doing great with his tent meetings, we would help him during the week, our trio would sing, and sometimes Elwood would have Bill bring the message. Tent meetings were very popular in those days. Sometimes our trio would sing during the tent meeting.

1959 we were expecting our 4th child. I was terribly sick with all my children, but this time there was a new medicine to combat the sickness so I was able to navigate, I was able to continue singing with the trio on television, but hard to believe these modern days, I was not allowed to be seen full body on the set. Mondane was sitting at the piano as she was our pianist and sang tenor, Dorla sang alto and, I was soprano lead and she and I had to stand behind the piano so that we could only be seen head and shoulders. **Paul Raymond was born Feb 27th 1960.** The doctor told me definitely no more children.

1960

BACK HOME AGAIN AFTER 14 LONG YEARS.

Six months later August 1960 I received word that my mother had a stroke, with financial help from the church I was able to return to England. I had to apply for passports, an American passport for Paul; I was taking him with me, he was too young to leave behind, I wasn't an American citizen so I had to have my British passport renewed. It was my first plane flight, needless to say I was very nervous. It was much more pleasant flying in those days, no security needed, I had 3 seats on the front left side of the plane, so that Paul could lie down across two of them. The attendant spent a lot of time playing with him; in turn he would take his little tongue and blow them a raspberry. I was able to have the attendant warm his formula in his bottle. He made a fuss, he never liked warm formula he preferred it cold. For my dinner I had Filet Mignon and all the trimmings. We landed at Heathrow about 7:00 a.m. My brother Jim, and Pop, my stepfather was there to meet me; from there we traveled to my Parent's home in Pocklington E. Yorkshire. It was a very long journey, consisting of, a little over two hundred miles, especially hard with a six-month old baby. It was great to finally see Jim and Pop again after fourteen years; we had all changed with the years.

We finally arrived home, it was so good to see my mother, I gave her a hug, and she kissed my cheek. I was very tired, and Paul was beginning to be fussy. We went to bed, but I had trouble sleeping, wondering how my other three children and Bill was faring, I was missing them already, but I soon became familiar once again with my surroundings, and began to enjoy being with Jimmy and my mother. Jimmy was married and had a lovely little girl a little over a year old named Carol. His lovely wife was named Mary. Of course it wasn't very long before Dolly came to visit with her new beau, Alf. Her husband Matt had passed away several years ago. On my first Sunday there my uncle Billy was visiting, and that evening, I mentioned the fact that I sure would like to have some fish and chips

There weren't any fish shops open around anywhere near Pocklington, or any other villages nearby. Of course there were no computers, Internet, or cell phones, to find out where there might be one open. My family didn't even have a phone. The nearest one was in a phone booth in Pocklington. Billy suggested a shop at Stamford Bridge; just a few miles away and he offered to go and check if it was open, He asked if I would care to go along with him. Of course I said "yes," and off we went. This was the uncle I dearly loved, who taught me to count and say my ABC's. We found the fish shop and it was open, we had trouble finding a parking place, and he had to drive to the next street and park on the side of the road. I stayed in the car while he went to buy the fish and chips.

MY ESCAPADE WITH THE LAW

He was gone a very long time and I began to worry. I waited a little longer and decided to go see what was keeping him so long. It was dark by this time and he had left his parking lights on so I turned them off and locked the car door as I left. I went to the end of the street and turned the corner, and as I looked up the street I could see by the streetlight that there was a long line (English version -queue) so I went back to the car and horrors! A policeman was walking around Billy's car. I walked up to him and before I could say anything he asked," is this your car?" "No," I answered, "It belongs to my uncle. Is there something wrong?" I was beginning to worry. "Why is the car locked? He asked, "Because I locked it," I replied, "and why aren't the parking lights on?" "Because I turned them off" "and why did you do that" he asked. I explained that I went to see what was keeping my uncle, since he left the parking lights on I turned them off, and I locked the door because I was leaving it.

He gave me a look like he was thinking how dumb she can be, then said, "don't you know it is against the law to park your car and leave it without the parking lights on and you must leave the door unlocked?" "No sir," I replied. "I didn't know." "Well don't let it happen again;" he said, and with that he walked away. Mother thought it was funny when we told her about it. She said, "It will probably be in the newspaper, Dumb American almost got herself arrested by a policeman at Stamford Bridge while waiting for the uncle to buy fish and chips." Later I read an article that said it was also the same law in Australia, laws have certainly changed since then.

It was great to be home again Billy, Jimmy, my cousin Maureen and I went to the seaside at Bridlington; we took Paul with us and went for a boat ride on the North Sea.

The highlight of my visit home was when Teddy came with his wife Joyce and daughter Denise. Fifteen years had passed since that fateful day when mother had called me aside to talk to me about leaving him and dad. It is hard for me to write this without tears, what a reunion we had and again as they took me to see my cousin Madge, she was the one who had helped Teddy find mother, she said she remembered where Dolly lived and from there, Dolly took them to be reunited with mother, Jimmy and Teddy became very close. I was a little disappointed because Teddy couldn't recall any remembrance of the years we lived together, I could vividly remember him, I wanted so badly to hug him, but back in those days the British were not into hugging, and he was now thirty years old, I was thirty four/

A VISIT WITH AN ENGLISH METHODIST MINISTER

Mother introduced me to a Methodist Minister she had been in touch with over the years. He told me about an American youth ministry that were having nightly services at the Butlin's Holiday Camp several miles from where mother lived. He suggested that we might like to attend. I got all the particulars from him, and suggested to Jimmy, that he, Mary, and I, might go one evening. He talked it over with Mary, she said she would love to go, and we made our plans for a night to attend. Mother offered to take care of Carol, and Paul. It was a lovely service, Jim, and Mary, enjoyed hearing some of the same Hymns and Gospel songs that we regularly recorded and sent to mother by mail; featuring Bill preaching, and Mondane, and I, singing. When the minister asked if there was anyone who would like to go forward to accept Jesus as Savior. I was so happy that Jim, and Mary, went forward and accepted Jesus, and on the way home we had such a great time singing all the hymns. Sad to say there was no place for follow up as practically all of the chapels had closed. Mother found one that was open for Sunday Service; it was sad because besides mother, the minister, and I. there were only 2 more persons attending

I talked with mother's doctor about her health and what were her possibilities for future life after having a stroke. It wasn't very good news, he said with care she had five years at the most. He said her heart was very weak and she had a leaky valve. The time passed very quickly. Bill and I corresponded by mail. I had planned to stay five weeks. I had been there three weeks when I received a letter from Bill saying there were problems in the church, Billy kept crying for his mommy, and they were having trouble consoling him. I now had to make a decision to stay the length of time I had planned, or change my plane reservation and go home to my family. I talked it over with mother before I made the choice to go home to my husband and children; she said she was OK with my decision. She was able to go with me when Jimmy took me to the travel agency in order to make arrangements to change the date if my flight. Jimmy told me years later that mother didn't let me know it, but she was really hurt, and wished I would have stayed, the sad part of it is, I was never to see her again.

CHAPTER
12

HOME AGAIN

We were all sad when Billy and Teddy came to take me to London Heathrow Airport. It was a long tiresome trip and Paul became a little fussy. I said good-bye with a few tears, finally at the airport I found my gate, and we hugged and promised to keep in touch, and Billy and Teddy left. My flight was delayed, and we were very late taking off, I was exhausted and Paul was irritable and tired. When we landed in New York I had missed my flight to Huntington W.VA I had flown TWA, and the airline official took me to the Travelers hotel and ordered a dinner for me, and milk for Paul, with anything else he might need. The next morning a limousine was waiting to take us to LaGuardia airport. What a difference in these modern times, if a flight is delayed we are lucky to get a blanket to try to make ourselves comfortable. I had to call Bill and let him know the new flight time; and thank goodness we had a phone at home.

It was a great homecoming; the children and Bill were pleased to see me. Billy clung to me like he was afraid I would leave again. There was some trouble with the Church. I will leave it at that. Bill prayed about the problems and handed in his resignation. He called the radio station and asked them to announce that he would be available for revivals and pulpit supply. Now began a time of trusting God and a testing of our faith. Bill began to receive calls for revivals in different churches. He now didn't have a regular salary, some of the churches he was called to were small, and he had to depend on the offerings that were taken during his revivals. One month he had been paid thirty six dollars for a two weeks revival we didn't have money for our household monthly payments there was forty dollars for the mortgage on the house and the electric and gas bill were due.

A DEFINITE ANSWER TO OUR PRAYERS

We prayed; I well remember I asked God to please provide the money. We owed exactly a hundred dollars. In my prayer I said it would bring a reproach on the name of Christ if we didn't pay our debts.

Bill was praying too. A couple of days later I went to the mailbox and there was one envelope. I took it in opened it and the Lord be praised there was a check for one hundred dollars, there was no letter or any message just a signed check. It was from a lady in Huntington W.VA her name and address was on the check. We had only met this lady once a few months before, she had called and asked if we would pick her up and take her to a revival Bill was preaching. We had never heard from her after we took her home after the service. I wrote and thanked her and explained how the check was an answer to our prayers and I have never heard from her from the day we received the check. She never acknowledged my letter. I call it my **second miracle**!

We continued to struggle with finances, Bill was often able to work for a friend who was a contractor but there came a recession and his friend had no work to offer. There were a few revivals that Bill was able to preach, but we struggled, because work was scarce in the contracting business and he didn't get many days work. Living in Kentucky during the recession wasn't easy. Once again we went on our knees and prayed.

January 1962

Bill received a call from the First Baptist Church of God in Columbus, Ohio and was invited to come to the church for a revival. The revival went on for three weeks; the congregation didn't want him to leave. This was the beginning of my having to stay home, while many times he would be gone from one to three weeks. Sheila was a great help to me on those days, helping take care of her three small siblings. It was great when Bill could get a call for a revival within driving miles of home. Mondane, Betty, and I could go with him, because it was usually requested that if possible we would be available to sing. By this time our car was on its last legs. We prayed that it wouldn't break down on the way to church and back. We never said anything but it was obvious when we arrived at the church the car was making an awful noise.

Next came our number three miracle, one afternoon there was a knock on our door, I opened the door, and there stood two dear friends, Earl Johnson, and his sister Beatrice Coldiron. Earl asked us to go outside, we followed them to our driveway, and behold there stood a shiny white four door Ford, which they presented to us, They explained that they had been noticing our poor old car, and had talked it over with Beatrice's husband Jess, and Earl's wife Frances; together they had bought the car. They then produced a box from their car, gave it to Bill to open, his eyes opened wide at the sight of a brand new suit, white shirt, and tie. Sadly all four are deceased, in fact so are all the people mentioned, except the younger members of my family, and friends. There is no other country in the world where one can find friends like these, especially those to whom God talks.

God says in His Word, (Paraphrasing,) that if we live for Him, and obey His commandments, He will supply our needs. When Bill first decided that he wanted to enter the Ministry, we knew that we would struggle financially, but never did we realize how God would supply our needs. I want to be clear about this, we can't just sit idly by, and expect miracles to come our way every time we have the smallest need. We must first do all we can, and then when we come to the impossible, God will step in. With four children to feed and clothe it wasn't easy, but we have never been hungry, or destitute, or ever had to ask for help. God always had ways of supplying, not our wants, but our needs.

Mother seemed to be doing fairly well, as long as she took it easy, she had to spend some time in the Hospital. She was able to write quite often, and was always sending packages for her grandchildren; there was always something for each of them. She sent a wire, with the money to buy Sheila's first bicycle.

JUNE 1962

I BECAME AN AMERICAN CITIZEN

In 1962 I decided it was time to become citizen. I had been back to England. I had enjoyed being there, and I would always have a place in my heart for the country of my birth, but I was now satisfied that America was my homeland. I had burnt my bridges, my four children and my husband were all American citizens, therefore it was time I joined them. I applied to the University of Kentucky to take a course on American Citizenship and

Government. I was accepted for a written course. I learned all about the 3 branches of government and everything that pertained to how this country was governed and much of its history. I made straight A's on my assignments, my thought was, and "I bet I know more about the laws and procedures of the running of this country than those who were born here." By the time I finished the course I felt I was ready to take my pledge. So on June 20 1962 I went before the Judge at Catlettsburg KY

I was very nervous there were three of us who were there to be sworn in. One of the others was a Greek Priest, the other a lady from Germany. I watched as the German lady took the oath, she was really interrogated, being asked if she was ever in East Germany, or was she ever a Nazi. By the time it was my turn I was so nervous. I wondered what kind of questions I would have to answer? I just hoped I could remember what I had learned from my studies. I worried for nothing, the only questions the judge asked me were, "Who was the first President of the United States, and what are the three Branches of Government?" I then had to renounce allegiance to Britain, and pledge my allegiance to America. I came away a proud Citizen and I have never regretted it

CHAPTER
13

1963

Bill received a call from the secretary of the First Baptist Church of God in Columbus Ohio, asking if he would be interested in becoming their Pastor, the present pastor had health problems and was resigning in July. He told them he didn't think he wanted to leave Ky; his mother was now a widow. The secretary said she would leave it for him to pray about, and left the number to call if he changed his mind. We talked it over and prayed about it and came to the realization that God was opening a door and we should walk through it. We had been praying for God to make a way for us as we still struggled with finances. The next morning he called the secretary and said he would take the church.

They didn't have to interview him as he had been with them in a revival the previous January. The revival had been scheduled for two week, it was so successful, they held it over for a third week, we made a trip to Columbus to make all the preparations and July 16th we moved into the parsonage. Now we had a beautiful church to pastor with a lovely parsonage and a decent weekly salary, and forty-seven members. It was quite a change moving from Kentucky to Ohio, and a change for Kathy and Sheila changing from a small town school to a large city school. Sheila was now sixteen and in high school. Kathy was seven and ready to go in third grade. Billy was five, I had to take him for his first day in school, I introduced him to his teacher, and he wouldn't turn loose of my hand. I finally had him sitting at his desk and turned to leave, telling him I would come for him after school, He began screaming and hanging on to my dress, the teacher took him to her desk trying to calm him down.

She told me to leave, as he would be all right as he got to know her. I left and I stood in the hallway listening to his screams, the janitor approached me and said very kindly, "ma'am, if you go back and get him you will never get him in school." I finally left and went home still hearing his screams in my ears. This went on for two days when he finally calmed down, he was OK and loved his teacher. Paul was three, he was alone now, because Kathy and Billy were in school, and he couldn't understand why he wasn't allowed to go to school. He was no trouble when it was his turn, he didn't want me to take him after the first day. I often wondered if the reason Billy acted that way was, because I had left him with his daddy when I went to England.

I must tell about MY NEXT MIRACLE, one Saturday close friends from Jackson Ohio, Jack, and Joann along with their six-year old son Jacky, were visiting with us. We had made arrangements to take a trip to Canada on the boat that left on Saturdays from Sandusky Ohio. We took Billy with us; and he and Jacky were very excited. Sheila kept Kathy and Paul. We had a pleasant drive and arrived in plenty of time to board the boat, it was a large ferryboat and there were about 100 or more people some with picnic baskets with food and drinks, evidently planning a picnic somewhere.

The boat docked at Peelee Island Canada, everyone had to leave the boat. Back then passports weren't necessary when arriving in Canada, but Customs Officers were waiting as we left the boat, we were asked what country we were born in. Of course I had to say England, the officer was very kind, he asked if I was an American citizen, I said "yes" "do you have your citizenship papers with you?" he asked. I explained that I didn't know I would have to show them. "Well," he said, you will be alright here as we are a part of the British Commonwealth, but when you try to get back in America you will be in trouble."

We left Peelee Island and went on into Canada. My trip was ruined, I thought what if they would keep me in Sandusky, while Bill went home and came back with my Citizenship Certificate. It was a little over a hundred miles from Sandusky to Columbus. I had a very pronounced British accent at the time, I thought, "if I say I was born near York, (not a lie, but deceitful) maybe they will think I am saying New York." I was a nervous wreck. Bill told me to stop worrying, if he had to go home and back to bring my Citizenship Certificate he wouldn't mind. I finally settled it in my mind; I told myself that God hates a liar. Saying I was born near York was not a lie, but it was deceitful and just as bad. So I made up my mind I just couldn't tell a lie, or be deceitful, if I had to stay in Sandusky with the customs officers, I should just have to trust God.

We had an interesting time looking around the city of Kingsville, not much different from the States. We found a restaurant, had lunch, and checked out the shops; also did a little sightseeing. We returned to the boat and we didn't stop off at Peelee Island on the way back. I had my mind made up that when I was asked where I was born I would just say England. When we finally arrived at Sandusky I thought, " I will soon know what will happen. We stood in line to leave, quite a number of people ahead of us. Jack, JoAnn and Jacky went ahead of us, then Bill and Billy, Now my time had come As I approached the Officer, I held my breath, he began to stutter, "Whe-a wha er wwwa ------, he kept stuttering and finally said, "What country are you a citizen of?" I said, "The United States of America." He said, "OK go through." That officer could only stutter, he could not ask me where I was born. JoAnn asked, "How did you get through?" We watched, and every one of the remaining people on board, was asked where they were born. I was the only one the officer couldn't ask.

After Paul entered school (I was thankful he was happy to go, no screaming and crying) I applied for a position at Lazarus Dept store, the largest store in Columbus. I was hired to work in the East Basement as an extra and soon became a regular and worked in the different departments as needed. These departments consisted of ladies, gents, and children's clothing, including teens. I loved my work and was mostly in children and ladies' departments. It worked out well as Bill was able to schedule his hours to coincide with the children's school hours.

Kathy loved taking the bus to town after school, to join me at Lazarus; she enjoyed helping fold clothes that the shoppers had left in a jumble. The church was doing well at this time, with a congregation of two hundred or more, not bad considering there were only forty-seven members when we first arrived. Bill was very well liked; he visited with some of the ministers of neighboring churches. The district supervisor of the Churches Of Christ in Christian Union, with headquarters At Circleville Ohio; approached Bill, and told him they would love to have him Pastor one of their churches. This was a much larger group than the Christian Baptist, where his ordination was held. Bill said he would have to pray about it, but as yet he didn't feel that God was finished with him at the Baptist Church.

The D.S. replied, " Let's just say this just isn't the time yet," that was something to think, and pray about for the future.

I was quite busy with the church; I organized a Junior Church for the children, during Sunday morning worship, also a Ladies Group that met once a week. I also joined with two of the members, Doris, and Patty to make up a trio, with Doris as our pianist, and tenor, Patty sang alto, and I sang lead soprano. We sang in all the services in our church, and were often asked to sing in other churches.

Good Friday 1965

A shock and despair

It was Good Friday; we had been to the grocery store, to do our weekly shopping, I was rushing to put everything away, because in less than an hour, I was scheduled to be at our monthly lady's meeting. Sheila had an envelope in her hand and was talking to her dad, and still in a hurry to leave; I didn't pay much attention to them. Bill came up to me insisting that I have something to eat before leaving, I told him it wasn't at all necessary, because there would be refreshments at the meeting. He kept insisting that I eat before I left; I was beginning to be aggravated, I asked him if he had a problem. Finally, he asked me to go upstairs with him, and I then figured something must be wrong, and I went upstairs with him, then I noticed that he had taken the envelope from Sheila. Holding the envelope in his hand, He said, "I know Sheila never opens our mail, likewise you or I never open hers."

He gave me the letter, and I was devastated, because it was from Jimmy, informing me that my mother had passed away, and had been cremated the previous Tuesday. She had died on the way to the hospital; Jimmy said he was with her in the ambulance. Sheila apologized for opening my mail; I assured her that it was OK. She said she kept looking at the envelope and would put it down, then pick it up, finally she said she felt that she just had to open it. I didn't answer the letter. I couldn't understand why they didn't wire me. I could have gone home. The sad part was that before he talked to me, Bill had called one of the elders of the church, to ask to have prayer for me, because he had to tell me of my mother's death. A meeting of the elders was called, and they decided to finance my visit home for the funeral, sadly it was too late, the letter took a week to arrive, the funeral was over, and mother had been cremated.

Our trio was scheduled to sing, at a special Easter Sunday Evening Service, at a Church of Christ in Christian Union. I told Bill I would have to cancel, as I couldn't sing after the news I had received, I said it was too much to ask, and I was too upset to sing. He talked to me awhile and finally convinced me that I could sing, I really didn't want to let the church and the trio down, so I went and was able to sing and put on a smile, but my heart was heavy.

I had no desire to go to England, since my mother had already been cremated. It was eight long years before I contacted any one again in England. Life went on, I was sad; there would be no more letters or packages from mother. I grieved for her and all I could think of were the times before I came to America when we didn't see eye-to-eye and quarreled a lot. It finally became easier as time passed, and I kept busy with the church activities. I began directing plays at Christmas, and our Junior Church was growing. Along with two of the other teachers I attended a year of classes for Children's Christian Evangelistic teachers. It qualified me years later to teach in a church's Christian School.

July 1968

We remained at the Christian Baptist Church until July 1968 at the end of the 5-year term. We were sad to leave but it was time to move on, we had gained lots of new friends along the way, many of them we still have contact with. After much prayer Bill met with the Churches of Christian Union District Superintendent, and it was agreed that if he would read one book that was mandatory, and answered all the questions, he could transfer his ordination from the Christian Baptist to the C.C.C.U. and so began another chapter in our life. We moved from the Baptist parsonage, and bought a house located in South Columbus. This was the same area, thus the children didn't have to change schools. In November 1968 Sheila married her first husband, Bob. We tried to discourage the marriage, because Bob was an alcoholic. Sheila was twenty-one, we could do nothing except pray and be there for her. Bill said he couldn't with a clear conscience perform the ceremony. Sheila was very hurt with his decision. Bill, knowing his own record with alcohol, he was afraid the marriage would end up in disaster. Bob lasted a few months before he let Sheila find out what he was like when he was under the influence of whisky. Sheila wanted children but had two miscarriage

CHAPTER
14

JULY 1970

Bill was accepted as the Co-Pastor with Pastor Rev. Guy Johnson at Valley View, Columbus Ohio; thus began our association, with the Churches of Christ in Christian Union . I continued working at Lazarus, at Christmas I was asked to supervise toys, a department was set up in the East Basement, it was a great area, a section was set up in the storage room where toys were packed ready to be mailed. I really enjoyed my Christmas promotion. I was in charge of the whole section with two women on the registers making sales and two in the packing area. I was very disappointed after Christmas sales were over and I was transferred back to salesclerk I inquired what was the reason I was no longer a supervisor and was told that because I didn't have a high school degree, I could never be a supervisor, no matter how experienced I was. I worked for 7 years in the East Basement as a salesclerk.

One day I was called into management and asked if I was interested in being transferred to the Cash Office. I was really thrilled to leave the sales floor. I was trained first to help count all money that came in from our downtown store plus the six branch stores. There were seven of us plus the supervisor and manager. We had to Ring a bell in order to enter the office and have a special badge. I was found trustworthy and was trained to run the machine that counted the paper money. One dollar bills were strapped in stacks of fifty, twenty and ten dollars, in stacks of hundred. I sometimes had a helper to strap them. I loved that job. The young man who trained me left the department and I was completely in charge. I decided it was time that I drive a car. I passed my written test, and applied for driving lessons. I took the lessons and passed with all A's then applied for my driver's license I took the driving test, and passed the first time, I even passed parallel parking. Now I was able to drive myself to work,

JULY 1972 Bill was asked to pastor Taylor Station CCCU church. He went one Sunday for a trial sermon and was accepted. There was a very nice parsonage; we rented our house during our stay at Taylor Station. We Made many new friends and enjoyed our new church. By this time, I had finally come to terms with losing my mother and decided it was time that I put aside all my hurt feelings, and renew my relationship with family in England. Since eight years had passed since April 1965. I didn't know if any of my relatives still remained at the same addresses.

I decided to take a chance on my stepfather still working at the milk factory. I sent a letter to him in care of the factory and asked if Dolly still live in Port Royal, Holme on Spalding Moor? I received his reply telling me that he was still working at the Milk Factory, and Dolly still lived at Port Royal. After receiving the letter from Pop as (I now refer to him) I wrote to Dolly, asking for an update on everyone. She wrote back and gave me all the news; Auntie Dora and Uncle Harry still lived on Back Lane. Dolly invited me to take a holiday and visit her.

June 1974

I talked it over with Bill and decided to take a couple of weeks' vacation from Lazarus and go back home again since Kathy and the boys were now grown, Bill was busy with the church, and Sheila was married. In June I booked my flight to London. I made arrangements with Pop to pick me up at Heathrow. He had a girlfriend named Betty and she came with him to meet me. After being introduced to Betty we left Heathrow about nine o'clock and began our long journey to Yorkshire. It was a harrowing trip we got lost; I saw a sign that said so many miles to Southampton. I mentioned that we were going south and should be going north. Pop found a place to turn around; I asked if he knew the way, he assured me he did. We drove another hour or so and I saw a sign 'To Welsh Border, now we were going west, I pointed to the sign and asked if he had a map, he had one in the glove compartment. I asked him to please give it to me.

I was becoming hungry and asked about stopping for food. He was beginning to be a little upset and told us in no uncertain terms that he was not stopping for food until we found the M1 Motorway. I read the map and found the route that would take us to the M1 it was an awfully long way. The roads were not as modernized back then as they are now. It was four p.m. when I had managed to guide him to the M1 and we finally had something to eat.

It was 10p.m. when we arrived at Dolly's. Billy was watching for us, and said, "Where have you been? Dolly has gone to your house Ted, to see if you have taken Kath there." About that time Dolly and Alf drove up. She hugged me and asked where in the world we had been. I had a great time when Teddy, Joyce, and family visited Dolly. We had a great reunion with aunts, uncles, cousins, nieces, and nephews. My brother Jimmy had recently remarried, Dolly rang him and told him I was visiting, they arrived, and Jimmy introduced me to his new wife June. It was great seeing Jimmy again, and getting to know June, with whom I became great friends as the years passed.

Then next morning Teddy and Joyce came, and took me Hornsea to see Madge. We had a lovely time visiting the Hornsea Pottery, after that, going across the fields to the North Sea Beach. It was difficult saying goodbye to Madge. The next day, Alf and Dolly decided they would love to see Little Deep Dale, I suggested we go there. They were delighted, and asked if I remembered how to get there, I assured them I did, and we set off. I was surprised how familiar the roads were, and easy to find after all these years.

When we finally arrived, they were horrified, and couldn't believe the roads and fields we had to travel from the Main road of Deep Dale to Little Deep dale. The house and outbuildings were still there; but were decaying, crumbling shells, not fit to chance going inside. We spent an hour or so, looking around, then back home to Dolly's where I was staying. Teddy and Joyce would visit every day, and we visited lots of relatives. It was a lovely three weeks, and time to go home; Pop along with Betty, drove back to London where we stayed overnight with Aunt Lil, then the next morning after saying goodbye to Aunt Lil, we went to Heathrow Airport, for the long flight to America and my family. Bill and the children were all happy to see mother home again. The next day we all sat for a family portrait, for which Bill had previously made an appointment.

1975 1978

WE RECEIVED OUR FIRST TWO GRANDCHILDREN

After much prayer, Sheila's husband, Bob, had decided to attend the church He went forward and accepted Christ. It was such a great blessing for Sheila no more drunken escapades; He had been sober for almost over a year. Sheila was now talking about adopting a child because Bob wasn't drinking. They were finally able to adopt two children, so we received our first two grandchildren; a lovely eleven-month-old baby boy Robert, and a beautiful little two-year-old girl Amy. We were now proud grandparents and loved going to visit and become acquainted with these two precious little ones; of course Robert became Bobby. During the years 1975 -1978 Bill didn't pastor any church, during which time we attended church at Taylor Station, the church where he had previously pastored.

I was still working in the cash office at Lazarus. I had always told Bill that I would appreciate it if he would never take a church that was too far away from Columbus to drive. I didn't want to lose my job at Lazarus. We depended on the help that my salary made. I always enjoyed being a Pastor's wife, I loved greeting the people and working with the children and all the activities of the church. I was missing all that, and I began to pray that Bill would receive an offer of a church, I even told God I would be willing to go anywhere, I would also give up my job if needed. I didn't tell Bill or anyone about my prayer, and let me tell you, don't ever make a promise to God unless you mean it.

About 3 weeks later I arrived home from work, Bill said he had a visitor that afternoon, I asked who it was, he said the District Super came to ask if he would take the CCCU church in Adrian Michigan. I asked, "What did you tell him?" He said, "I told him I didn't think so, as you always said you wouldn't want to quit your job at Lazarus." "What did he say?" I asked. "He told me to pray about it and call him after he talked it over with me.

My heart was beating rather fast as I listened and thought about my prayer. I told Bill, he should call the D.S. and tell him we will go, and then I told him how I had prayed. The next day he called the D.S. and told him we would take the church.

A few weeks later I gave my notice at Lazarus, everyone was sad to see me go, I had been in the cash office 7 years, 14 total years with the store. We made arrangements to move into the parsonage at Adrian Mich. The boys and Kathy were on their own Billy (now insisted on being called Bill) agreed to live in our home until we returned. We moved into the parsonage and became acquainted with the members. As we settled in our new home, we missed our grandchildren, but Sheila made sure they didn't forget us; she brought them often for a weekend visit. I begged her to let me keep Amy for a week but like all new mothers she couldn't bear to leave her. During the first few months of our stay in Michigan we had to make several trips to Ashland Ky. First, Bill's brother in law, Roy, passed away on Sept. 12th 1978. Then a week later on the 20th Roy's wife, Bill's sister Mag, died in the doctor's office from a heart attack.

Granny had been living with us for quite a while, she didn't want to move to Michigan she told us she was 92 and wouldn't be here much longer an she didn't want to leave Ashland Ky. We tried everything to talk her into going with us, but she said no, and packed and rang for Billie Jean to come and take her back to Ashland. We went to Ashland t [o say goodbye to her, and she was very feeble, I told Bill as we were on the way to Michigan, we would never see her again alive. I cried all the way there. That day came a few weeks later Granny ha left this world. I had lost the best mother in law a woman could ever hope for. We made the journey to all the funerals. Sadly, one by one, our relatives were leaving us.

The following are events that developed, from my decision to being willing to leave Lazarus, and accepting to go where God would lead us was almost unbelievable. One of the members of our new church informed me of a program that the government was offering, a complete business course. Amazingly it was to be with pay and consisted of typing, shorthand lessons, filing, and the correct way of answering a business phone call. I signed up for the course and was accepted. I was also able to take a G.E.D. test and was told if I passed the test, I would have a high school education and be presented with a High School Diploma. I knew that my British seventh grade education was pretty close to an American tenth grade. My son Paul and his friend Rick came up to Adrian one weekend and tried to teach me Algebra, Ha, ha, they might as well have tried to teach me a foreign language in a weekend. I finished the year business course and made straight A's. I took the G.E.D. test and was informed that my grade was one of the highest 25% in all America.

1979

Kathy came on a visit to, introduce her new friend Tom Buchanan, of whom we heartily approved. We enjoyed a lovely weekend becoming acquainted with him. They were married the following November, and our son Bill married the lovely Meg (Margaret) Owens after a rather long engagement. The most amazing facts about our move to Michigan are as follows. A few weeks after I gave my notice at Lazarus, there was a theft in the cash office; someone on the inside was the guilty person. The cash office was dismantled and closed, from that time on, all the monies that came in, were sent to the bank to be counted. If I had stayed I would have had no job; unless there was an opening somewhere else in the store, and there were no business course lessons offered in Ohio.

1981-1985

We stayed in Michigan for a three-year term. When we moved back to Columbus I applied for work at Lazarus. Even though I now had a high school diploma, they had no openings. My daughter Kathy informed me that Farmers Federal Auto Insurance Company had moved to Dublin Ohio and they were hiring. The next day I drove to Dublin and applied for a position at the Insurance Company. I was interviewed and told I would receive a phone call if they could use me. I became a little anxious the next few days waiting until the call finally came. We settled back in our home. On Feb 16th 1981 I was hired as a Quality Controller, which consisted of stuffing envelopes with several special forms, then another person would take them down to the mailroom. It was quite boring but I really worked hard at it until several months later I was promoted to the change section.

My very first experience using a computer was making changes of coverage on auto insurance. From change I moved to New Business, taking application forms from Underwriting and printing from the forms to the computer. In those days there was no Internet, everything was typed on a small computer, that entered an enormous computer ending up on a reel, that was taken down to Data Processing every afternoon; The large computer had to be initialized once a month. I worked there eleven years and moved up to O.C.C .an assistant supervisor. After five years, we were able to receive profit sharing every spring. Sad to say Sheila's husband had turned to the alcohol again and began abusing Sheila. He finally was arrested for an altercation with a mailman, was arrested, and sentenced to Prison in Ashland Kentucky. Sheila finally divorced him.

Bill was accepted as Associate Pastor with Pastor Lee Tabor at Reeb Ave. Christian Union Church in Columbus Oh, and served until 1983, when due to his health he decided to retire and draw early retirement. During this time at Reeb Ave I directed Junior Church, and directed my first Christmas Play, which was a great success. 1982 we had visitors from England; my niece, Denise, and husband, Dean, came for two weeks. It was lovely to see them, we took them to visit our relatives in Kentucky, also to Lake Erie, it was sad to say goodbye when they left. We had quite a pleasant two years until Bill had a problem with his health and had to go to the doctor for tests, because of problems with swallowing, after which he entered Riverside Hospital for surgery on his esophagus.

For a time he had to take it easy. It was great to be back in Ohio. On January twenty eighth 1983 we were blessed with a grandson, Andrew, Paul's son. He was a real joy; I loved the times when I got to help take care of him. Bill's health began to improve, and he was taking it easy and spent some Sundays visiting some of the churches we previously pastored. Christmas Day1983 Herstle passed away, that was a sad Christmas. We went to Kentucky to be with Jin at the funeral. Jin was nearing age eighty, and she and Herstle were like mother and father to me, I dread the day we will have to say goodbye to Jin.

April 1984 I received a call from my brother Jimmy, his wife June, had passed away, she was only 44 years old, and died from kidney failure.

Bill and I talked it over and we decided I should go to England to be with Jimmy. I made arrangements with my manager at work to be gone a week, and left the following day. I flew to Manchester, where my brother Ted, and wife Joyce, was there to meet me. We went directly to Jimmy's house where I made foolish request; I wanted to go to the funeral parlor to see June. (*The only British funeral I had ever attended in England was my brother Raymond's (Poggy's) funeral, and he was kept at home in his little coffin until the burial.*) Teddy, and Jimmy agreed to take me.

I shall never forget the experience of that night. We arrived at the funeral parlor and asked to see June Marshall. We were taken to a cold room, and asked to wait; after about ten minutes we were taken in a colder room where June lay in a coffin. I have never in my life seen anyone look the way June looked. Her face was black, blue, orange, and, purple. The bags under her eyes were stretched down to the bottom of her face. None of us said a word as we turned away and left. Teddy and Joyce went back to Jimmy's house; and then they left to go back to their home in Hull.

I stayed with Jimmy, and as we sat on his sofa he suddenly said, "I don't want to go to heaven if June didn't go." I told him he shouldn't feel that way because we don't know what is in a person's heart, and it isn't our place to judge. I recalled the time that he had once accepted Christ in 1960 when I was home, and Jimmy, his first wife Mary, and I, had gone to an American Youth Christian Service that was being held in a Butlin's Holiday Camp. At the end of the service they went forward and accepted Jesus into their lives. We had a time of rejoicing as we drove back to mother's house, singing all the songs that Mondane and I had sung on tape and mailed to them.

We still couldn't get over seeing the condition of June's face. I asked Jimmy if he had any videos that he had taken when I had previously visited. He found some, and brought some of them out. As we watched the videos it helped to see June as she normally looked. We enjoyed remembering the good times we had together, then I asked Jimmy if he would like to pray, he said he would, and we then knelt by the sofa and prayed. After the prayer we sat back on sofa, and I asked if he felt better, he said he felt so much better and at peace. He told me that every morning, while June was fixing breakfast, she always listened to the tapes of Mondane and I singing, and some of Bill's messages.

He also told about two or three weeks before June died, he felt like asking her to pray, but he was too embarrassed to ask her, how sad, it made me so thankful that I was an American. (I was reminded how shocked I was when I first arrived in Kentucky, and heard people talking about God and Jesus so freely.) Jimmy and I talked for quite a while and I told him no one, only God knows what is in a person's heart and we must not judge.

At the funeral, which was held at the funeral Parlor, no obituary was read, the Minister said a prayer and read the Twenty Third Psalm. Jimmy had asked if I could say a few words. The Minister agreed, I can't recall much of what I said, but I do remember saying that June was not only my sister in law but she was my friend, and I along with other friends would miss her, and Also spoke a few words to Jimmy and to June's family. After the service we went back to Jimmy's house where Joyce and I had fixed some refreshments. June's mother came to me and thanked me for speaking at the funeral. She said she felt so much better after I spoke, I was so glad I agreed to speak as it was such a cold informal service. I had become used Funeral Services in America, with friends coming to view the loved one whom the undertaker had made to look peacefully asleep. I hated to leave Jimmy, but I was glad to be back in America.

CHAPTER

15

1985

Bill's health had improved, and he was asked to be Associate Pastor at Bible Community Church, with Rev. Ed Adkins. We were there until 1989 during which time I was choir director, I also began teaching first and second grades at our Christian School, and supervised chapel every Wednesday. I separated them by grades and had kindergarten thru end grade, third grade thru fifth, and sixth grade thru high school. I also directed a Christmas play for Junior Church every year. I loved working with the children and the high school teenagers it was good to see Bill being able to be back in the pulpit, he and Rev. Adkins had been good friends down thru the years and enjoyed working together.

In July we had a lovely surprise, it was Wednesday the twenty fifth 1985 we were expecting that everyone would be there for prayer meeting. No one was in the Sanctuary when we arrived. We looked around and wondered why no one was there. Finally Pastor Adkins came and told us to go with him to the dining room. Surprise, everyone was gathered there to celebrate our fortieth wedding anniversary. Pastor Adkins was laughing and I looked at him to see why he was laughing, and I saw he had a nylon stocking pinned to his slacks. I said, "Oh No" Bill had told him about an experience I'd had at work one morning. This is the embarrassing story.

One day at work we were waiting at the elevator, on the way to the cafeteria for a break, when one of the girls asked me what was wrong with my foot. I looked down and saw something on my shoe, I got hold of it and pulled, and kept pulling, it was a pair of tights. I had worn the same slacks that day as I'd worn the day before. Evidently at bedtime I had pulled off slacks and tights together, and didn't notice them as I put them on the next day'

1986 - 1989

KATHY AND TOM VISIT TO ENGLAND,

JANUARY SEVENTH 1986. My second mother, Bill's sister passed away this was a sad time for us. Granny and Jin will be missed, because they were closer to me than my own mother. I had only lived with my English family for nineteen years, and by 1986 I had lived with my American family 40 Years. On both sides of the Atlantic Ocean the families of our generation were leaving us one by one.

On a lighter side, June the twentieth 1986 Kathy and Tom informed us that if we could manage it, they would like to go with us of us on a visit to England. This was an excellent time to go because we had been so sad losing granny and Jin. I was anxious to see Jimmy and Teddy, not forgetting Dolly. We made arrangements to go in June, usually a good month to visit England, because the weather is usually favorable. We flew into Heathrow, where Teddy, Joyce, Jim, and his daughter Elaine met us. Bill and I rode with Teddy and Joyce, Tom, and Kathy rode with Jimmy and Elaine. We all went to Jimmy's home, then after a rest from the long journey from London to York, Ted and Joyce went home to Hull. They promised to return two days later with Dean and Denise, to go to Wales to meet Dean's parents.

I had never been to Wales so it was a new experience for me. Wales is located in the south west of England. It is a beautiful place the mountains were covered with rhododendrons. Dean's parents lived in what was called a long house. In olden days the animals lived in one end of the house, and it had been remodeled and the animal part was now an extra bedroom and bathroom. It was a very lovely, interesting house, with quite a large back yard where Dean's mother raised goats. The little goats were lovely to watch, they were constantly jumping from one fence to another, and they were very entertaining. There was so much to see and do in Wales, there were a large number of castles, and most of they were open to the public. We went through several of them they were awesome, such beautiful places, I had read many books with stories about castles from the olden days, and I found that the books I had read described them amazingly, Tom and Kathy were intrigued with them.

One of the castles was partly destroyed, because it was hundreds of years old. It was the Caearnafon Castle. Hundreds of years ago England and Wales were at war, when the war finally ended a treaty was to be signed between them, but the only way that Wales would consent to end the war and sign the treaty, was for England to agree that the first son born to the Royal family was to belong to Wales. The child would become the Prince of Wales. At a certain age *(I don't remember what age)* he was taken to Wales for what was called the investiture. I did read that Prince Charles was taken to the castle at the age of twenty, and crowned by Queen Elizabeth for his investiture. On one of the walls was a list of names of men who had served in one of the old wars. Bill was excited about it, because one of the names on the list was John Lewis Price, the name of his father, (Papaw Price.) it was a lovely visit, and in the evening Dean and his father prepared a barbecue. We stayed two days and nights, and saw so many lovely sights, then back to Jimmy's for Kathy, and Tom, Bill, and I, went home with Teddy, Joyce, Dean, and Denise.

Kathy and Tom spent the remainder of the two weeks at Jimmy's. Bill and I spent some time with Dolly and Alf. And some time with Ted and Joyce, then every day we would all meet at Jimmy's. It was a great time we went to Scarborough, Which is the largest beach on the North Sea, where my cousin Kathleen lives. Teddy and Joyce took Tom, Kathy, Bill, and I, to Hornsea (also on the North Sea) to see Madge. Kathy would stare at Teddy. She couldn't believe how much he looked like her brother Bill. I told her not to be so surprised, after all he is my brother. Until Jimmy had a problem with his heart, he had worked as double deck bus driver. He was able to obtain permission to take us to the bus garage and from there, take us for a ride through York. This was something new for Kathy and Tom. Bill was already familiar with them, having ridden on them with me during the war.

It was a lovely time, Kathy fell in love with her uncle Jimmy, she was fascinated with her uncle Teddy, in fact she loved all the relatives but Jimmy and Dolly were her favorites. They all *(Except Dolly and me)* went for a walk around York Wall, which is 5 miles around what is left of it. Dolly and I went to the Museum Gardens and lazed in the sun; the weather was beautiful the whole three weeks. Tom and Jimmy played some of their tricks on me. Jimmy had finally got someone to help him with his mischief. One night after we had visited some of the shops in York and of course we had fish and chips. We were all tired that evening, we sat and talked and I was ready for bed, but no one was interested, I asked Bill if he was ready for bed but he said he would just wait till the rest of them went. So I went upstairs and prepared to get in bed, pulled the covers back and a Huge and I mean HUGE spider ran on the sheet. I screamed and jumped away from the bed, and heard loud laughter at the bottom of the staircase, where they were all standing, waiting for me to scream, knowing I am terrified of anything that crawls.

On one of the nights Bill and I stayed with Dolly and Alf, we had made arrangements to meet Jimmy, Tom, and Kathy, at Jimmy's house. The next day when we arrived, we got out of the car, and I went to the front door, and knocked, no one answered, I tried the door and it was locked, I was fussing and said they could have at least left a note on the door to let us know where they had gone, I went around to the back of the house but no one was there. About fifteen minutes after they figured we had been annoyed enough, they come out of the barn where they had hidden the car and themselves laughing their heads off. I was so glad Tom and Kathy had such a good time. All good things must sometimes come to an end. That was the best of my visits home, except, 1960 when I saw my mother for the last time. It was time to go back home to America we had the same chauffeurs going back as when we arrived, to take us back to London, then on home to Columbus, Ohio.'

1987 was a pretty good year, Bill I were kept very busy at Bible Community Church, Bill was happy working with Rev. Akins, I, with school every day, Choir practice on Wednesday evening before the Prayer Service and directing the choir during Sunday morning Service. Beginning in September we began have practice for our School children's Christmas play, I still have pictures of some of our plays, and keep in touch with my pupils on face book. So many great memories, so many friends, that we have known and loved. God has really blessed our lives. I have been able with God's guiding, to accomplish so many things that I could never have done in England. I tell the Lord many times, " I know where You brought me from and I know where I am today, we are so" blessed. My assistant choir director Rita, and I sometimes visited the hospitals when a member was ill, usually we would take flowers to the ladies, the men patients we left for the pastors to visit

January seventh 1988 Bill and Meg presented us with a grandson, Michael Fredrick Price. He was such a lovely little boy. He reminded me so much of my sweet little Poggy, with his chubby cheeks and lovely smile. I loved it when Meg and Bill would bring him for me to take care of him for a few hours. How I love my Grandchildren, they are all so precious. Our years at Bible Community were very pleasant, it was good to see Bill feeling much better and able to preach and visit the sick. He and Pastor Adkins worked very well to together. The congregation loved it when Bill preached. He had a great sense of humor. I always have a terrible time sitting still, I have to be doing something with my hands, and if we travel in the car I twiddle my thumbs, and this one Sunday morning I did the unthinkable.

I'm almost ashamed to tell it, and I promise I have never done anything like it since. I was enjoying Bill's sermon, and my hands were getting restless, I had on a string of beads, which I began playing with, and I put them on the end of my nose. Bill took one look at me, I could tell he was trying to keep from laughing and he said, "Sister Price it is hard enough to preach without you having your beads on the end of your nose." I'm ashamed to say the whole church was trying to keep from laughing. After the end of the service, every one of the ladies got together and made their plans. During the evening service when Bill raised his head after reading his scripture and praying, as he looked up at the congregation every lady had a pair of beads on her nose. The look on Bill's face was precious. That is the only time I ever did anything naughty in church, now you know I am definitely not perfect!

I continued working in the school and chapel; I had such a great time with the children. Pastor Adkins allowed me an hour every day to give the children time away from class. The girls enjoyed singing and were interested in learning music. I taught them how to read music and to play the notes and scales on the piano. I even had a knitting class. With the boys it was quite different, they liked games so we had a game with the Bible. I had them sit in the back pew, then I would choose a scripture, book, chapter, and verse, and the first to find it had to read it and if it was correct they moved up a pew and the one who reached the front pew was the winner. They also loved discussions, and often tried to trip me up with question they thought I would not be able to answer. Sometimes I would take them outside to play ball.

I was always having something stupid happen to me. I had a bad back, and one day as usual, young Bill had beaten me to the bathroom, I was running late, and on the way to work as I parked the car and got out, and as I began walking into work and I thought something happened to my back. I was limping, and I thought one of my legs felt shorter than the other. When I got to work the first thing my co-workers asked me if I had a problem? They looked me over and laughed, I had on odd shoes, they were both white, but one was a high heel shoe and the other a flat heel. As Pastor's wife usually when it was found that I could take a joke, the men would always find something to tease me about. One of the other ministers always called me English Hillbilly.

I also get lost easily

1989 -1993

Once again, Bill was approached by our D.S. The Grove City, Ohio Christian Union Church was having serious problems. A new pastor was needed and the D.S. felt that Bill would be the only one he could think of who would be willing, with God's help to deal with the situation. We were living in the North end of Columbus, twenty miles north of Grove City. And because at present Bill was Co-pastor if a Non-denominational Church, as an Associate Pastor, it would be expected that we would resign as soon as possible, because we were, and still are, members of the Churches of Christ in Christian Union. Bill had never refused to help any Church that was in trouble, in fact a few that he Pastored have been needy churches that he was able to help. He told the D.S. he would do his best, but after he found out the facts, he was really worried, but his theory was. *'With God, all things are possible.'*

These are the facts. The church bank account had a mere total of eight dollars, the former Pastor's salary had not been paid for two months, and the utility payments were due. Bill came home with the news that the church would not be able to pay him any salary until all debts were paid, and the bank account was replenished. There was no help offered from Circleville Church Extension. Bill was to inform the D.S. when and how he was going to would proceed with a plan to remedy the situation. We had helped other churches in trouble, but this was the worst we had ever known. Others had been lacking membership, low number of members, or low on finances, but this was the Granddaddy of them all.

We prayed and talked it over and prayed some more, then decided the first item on the list was as follows, much prayer, because it was a certain fact that we needed a miracle. Only through help from God could it be accomplished, next item, the former Pastor would be allowed to remain in the parsonage until his salary was paid in full. Then let it be known that the new Pastor will be Bill Price, next obtain a list of names of present members, also as many names of previous members as possible. Send them a notice of the date and time when the new pastor will be charge of Sunday Morning Services, and Wednesday Evening Services. The utility bills would be brought to the attention of those attending the first Sunday morning service and a special offering taken to help pay for them.

The D.S. was pleased with the plans, and we prayed a lot because we couldn't manage all these plans without God's help. The first Wednesday evening service was in November, we drove from Columbus to Grove City; Bill had the keys to the church. It was snowing and we went inside and waited and no one came the weather was getting really bad. We were just preparing to leave when an elderly gentleman came in. He had seen the lights on in church, and because the weather was so bad he decided to stop in. He was on his way to another church much further away. Bill welcomed him with a handshake, and introduced us as Bill Price the new Pastor and wife Kathleen I told him good evening and shook his hand, left the gentleman introduced himself as Bro Fritz Baugus, Bill explained that this was the first service of the new pastorate, but it appeared no one had braved the storm.

They sat in the back of the church, while I decided to softly check the piano, it was terribly out of tune, and very old, it was plain to see that it would need to be tuned, and possibly replaced when it could be afforded. The carpet was in bad shape, it was already beginning to be threadbare in lots of places, which were badly in need of repair. I was already seeing some of the needs. Bro Fritz Baugus left, we turned out the lights and made our way home slowly, because of the deepening snow. So ended our first Wednesday evening at Grove City Church.

The following Sunday morning the snow had stopped, and the roads were clear. It was encouraging to see some people coming in we both stood at the door to welcome them most were members but there were a few who had heard the news and already knew us and some of them wanted to help. Our new friend Fritz Baugus walked in, he had decided to come and help revive the church. He and Bill became great friends

The service was great and Bill out did himself with God's assistance, and preached a wonderful message. There was a small crowd, an offering was taken for utility debts, I don't remember the total, and I assume the records should still be at the church. This was a great beginning, thanks to the help and Grace of God and the people. The congregation began to grow, Bill was very well liked and was an awesome preacher.

Many times I was amazed at how, when he first felt the calling, he was not a very good reader, he admitted he had bad grades at school and had no high school education, I knew it all had to have come from God, I knew the hours he spent in prayer and studying his bible. What an amazing God we have. As the attendance began to grow, it still amazed me how God taught Bill to read well; also he was also able to deal with the financial situation. *(He still depended on me to deal with our personal finances.)* The former Pastor had been reimbursed for all his unpaid salary, and having thanked everyone, said goodbye, and moved from the parsonage.

Some of the women at the church readied the parsonage for us to spend the weekends in Grove City, which made it so much easier, and cheaper than driving from north Columbus twice a week. Now he was able to be paid a small salary, it was a great help that thanks to the Great God that we serve, I had a good paying job at Farmers Auto Insurance *(I often look back on our life, and am amazed at how Bill changed from a WW 11 alcoholic veteran, to a Minister trained by God. When he turned his life over to God he never had another drop of alcohol, never had to be treated for alcoholism, never again had any desire for it. To become a well-known, and well thought of preacher, only came by much prayer, fasting, and studying.)*

By the time two years passed, the church was out of debt, we were averaging an attendance of eighty to 100 every Sunday. The carpet had been repaired and the pews padded, the platform remodeled, a new piano was bought, ceilings were installed in the basement and Bill helped build nice large storage building on the church lot, and there was twelve thousand dollars in the bank. Our daughter Kathy filled the need of a pianist. I was Junior Church Director, and was voted in as Missionary President. The church was able to pay Bill a weekly salary of a hundred and twenty five dollars. Everything that was bought for the church had been bought with cash only. Bill had informed the board that there would be no credit used for anything. It was amazing the help that was offered free of charge for repairs.

We had good music and singing as part of Sunday services, often with popular groups of singers. Kathy and our grandson Bobby and I, would sometimes sing, Once we were singing Thank you for your Blessings, I was supposed to sing 'There's food on my table and shoes on my feet,' and instead I sang 'There's shoes on my table and food on my feet' and I wondered why Kathy and Bobby became amused, but kept on singing, because I never realized what I had done. I was embarrassed when they told me, but I felt a little better when someone remarked, "that shows that you are just like the rest of us, and not perfect." God was really blessing the church; the attendance was growing and then comes bad news.

1991 two more loved ones have gone

Sunday March eighteenth Dolly rang me to say my fifty-four years old brother, Jimmy, had a massive stroke, and wasn't expected to live. I talked with Bill about going to be with Jimmy, he said he was sorry he couldn't go with me. Monday, I called and asked my manager if I could have a week off, because I needed to go to England to be with my brother, because he had a massive stroke and was expected to die before the middle of the week. I was granted a week off with pay. I made arrangements to fly to Manchester on Tuesday evening the nineteenth. Teddy and Joyce met me at the airport, and we traveled the 60 odd miles to York, and made our way to the hospital.

Jimmy was in the intensive care unit with a nurse by his bed, and he was unconscious. Teddy and Joyce left after about two hours, Teddy was beginning to wear down, he had a pacemaker for his heart. I decide to stay with Jimmy. Teddy couldn't understand why I wouldn't leave. I couldn't let him die alone. (*I still had en's got over Poggy's dying alone at the age of five.*) Jimmy's son in law Audie, (Carol's husband) came to the hospital, and we both sat by Jimmy's bedside. I wondered if he knew I was there, I took his hand, and asked him to squeeze it if he knew, but there was no response, then as I was ready to turn away, I saw a tear appear from his eye, sometimes I wonder if it meant he knew, but I believe that he did, because I know; 'All things are possible with God if we believe.'

6:30 a.m. Wednesday morning, I said goodbye to Jimmy, I kissed the top of his head, Audie, and I watched him take his last breath, *(it was like watching my own child leave me. We were so close, even though we lived 3,000 miles away. (When he was in his teens, mother used to write to me and ask, "would you write to Jimmy, because you could always reason with him, and handle him much better than I could.")* The funeral had to be the next day, which was Thursday, because it was Easter, and everything and in England was closed from Good Friday to Easter Monday .the funeral was so different from our American funerals.

I was standing between Dolly and Teddy, next to them were Audie and Carol, and several other relatives and friends, The minister read the Twenty third Psalm and said a prayer, no words of comfort, I stood there and tears were nearly blinding me, wishing I had someone to put an arm around me, no one else seemed to shed a tear. I really can't remember leaving the funeral parlor or where we went after leaving .I suppose I went to Hull with Teddy and Joyce. There was no burial because he was to be cremated.

The next day we went to visit Madge and Dolly before I returned home. I had to be back at work the following Tuesday. I don't have much recollection of my journey home, after I said goodbye to everyone it was like I was in a daze. Exactly a year later Phil rang to say Dot passed away with a heart attack, she and Jimmy were the same age. I couldn't possibly go to the funeral, but we were able to send flowers along with condolences.

September 1991 at the age of 65 I retired from Farmers Insurance. I would have stayed on a few more years but the company was moving back to Los Angeles, California and some of the employees moved with them. I was able to retire with a reasonable pension, and my Social Security. I would have more time to help at the church. Mondane and husband Bud visited at times, Mondane and I always enjoyed singing together again. I enjoyed directing a Junior Church Christmas Play, with children ages three through twelve, the children were so excited because most of them had never had a part in a play, it was a great success. I was happy because now I had more time to plan activities for the children. It was awesome knowing that because of everyone praying and believing, because God was working to make these accomplishments.

March 8th 1992

Sheila married Paul Tulloch, a retired Columbus Police officer. She was very happy being married to Paul for with him, her life had become so much better. March fifteen 1993 Bill and I were able to take a trip to England, Thanks to a very generous gift from Sheila's husband Paul. At this time the church was in great shape so it would be good to have a three weeks' vacation. We made our reservations to Manchester, also arranging to have someone meet us at the terminal, we then said goodbye to Sheila, Paul, and our other children, Kathy, Bill, and Paul. We enjoyed a smooth flight, and after going through customs we were met by Teddy, and Joyce; then headed to Yorkshire.

We had a great time visiting relatives, We Stayed part time with Teddy and Joyce and Dolly. Of course we visited Madge. We sadly missed Jimmy, and Dot. My British and American families were becoming smaller in number every year. We had a lovely time staying with Teddy, and Joyce, and having them taking us around the City of Hull, where I formally lived, before leaving England. One day Bill asked Teddy if he would mind taking us to the Pier, because he would love to reminisce about the many times during the war, he would arrive on the ferry, and after landing, and walking through the exit, he knew I would be waiting, to take him to my home at 6 Wilberforce Villas Rosemead ST. Hull to stay with mother, my two little brothers, and me, for the weekend, not forgetting sitting on a bench at the Pier, was the place where he proposed to me.

When we arrived, sadly there was no ferryboat or pier but we could look out over the river Humber that sailed from Hull E. Yorkshire to New Holland Lincolnshire and exchange memories of those long ago week ends when I met him at the pier, The days seemed to pass so quickly, and soon we make ready to leave, we visited as many as possible but the time came to say goodbye, pack our bags and once more be on our way to Manchester and board our flight to Ohio by way of New York.

September 11th 1993

Paul and Lori presented us with a beautiful granddaughter Rebekah Kay; SHE MISSED MY BIRTHDAY BY 5 DAYS, now I could really enjoy my retirement, because Bill, and I. had the privilege of baby-sitting. Bill was slowing down, he began having more problems with his health, and board members were considering that maybe a younger man would be needed to pastor the church. If this were going to happen it would be a hard decision for Bill. We had a meeting with the first elder, and he thought we should consider these facts, and during the remainder of the month, the board had chosen a young minister from the College to replace Bill, a very bad and hurtful decision. Apologies and regrets were made to Bill sometime later, but the damage was done.

About a year later we visited the church for a special service, to show we had no hard feelings, there were about 35 people in attendance I will leave it at that. In November we moved our membership to Beacon of Hope. Grove City Church was Bill's last Pastorate. He worked as much as possible with Pastor Kevin, (*my former Junior Church member) as* associate and helped with visitations as he was able.

1994 Tragedy Strikes

May third 1994 after two years of a happy marriage, Sheila's husband Paul Tulloch, a well-known Columbus police officer, was killed. He was driving home in his Honda car on a bridge close to Riverside Hospital Columbus, Ohio when a man in a delivery van crossed three lanes of traffic, and hit Paul head on. I can't remember where I had been, but when I arrived home the police were in my driveway waiting to take me to the hospital. Bill had already taken Sheila to the hospital. Paul didn't have a chance. Sheila was devastated, it was a very large funeral, and he was a well-known State Patrol Officer and a veteran; Sheila was years overcoming her grief.

We went to the Columbus, Ohio Court House with Sheila for the hearing of Paul's death. (I *don't remember the date*) the charge to the driver of the van was a fine of two hundred dollars and his driver's license was revoked for one year. November ninth 1994 my cousin Kathleen rang me to say Dolly has cancer in the last stage. Bill and Meg had divorced. I was sad but Bill wanted a large family and Meg was happy with just Michael. I love Meg, and she will still be a part of our life; she knows I will always be there for her and Michael.

1995

February thirteenth 1995 Dot's husband Philip rang to say Dolly passed away; I was devastated, because so many of my relatives were gone. Once more I made arrangements to fly home for the funeral, thankfully Sheila took good care of her dad while I was gone, his health was failing again. I flew into Manchester on the fourteenth; Teddy and Joyce were at the airport to meet me. We stopped at the home of Dolly's son Lesley, and wife Dorothy, where Dolly lay in state; Les asked if I wanted to see Dolly, of course I said yes. She looked so peaceful, as I said my last goodbye.

The funeral was in the Church on the Hill at Holme on Spalding Moor February seventeen. The burial was in the graveyard behind the church. There was reception and refreshments at the Cross Keys Inn. I returned home on the twenty-first. May the ninth I received word my stepfather Ted Marshall passed away. On July twenty sixth 1995 our children had a fiftieth anniversary reception for us at Bible Community Church. It was a great time, so many friends and relatives visited, also messages from so many of our friends and relatives in Kentucky. Lots of calls from England, Teddy, and Joyce sent us a sugar and creamer set with fifty written on them in gold.

1996

CHAPTER

17

1996

April 24th 1996 Bill and Rhonda Helber were married, Rhonda had three children, Thirteen years old Todd, and twelve years old twins, Thad, and Dawn thus Bill now had his large family, and was blessed with three new grandchildren. July second 1996, Bill was back in Riverside Hospital to have his stomach valve opened. July ninth Joyce rang me; with the news that Teddy was in hospital for open-heart surgery, a double by-pass, and two valves to be replaced. The surgeon told Joyce that Teddy came through the surgery, but they were keeping him sedated, because he was still in danger.

July 25th 1996 the call came, Teddy had passed away, July twenty-ninth he was cremated. I couldn't go to his funeral and leave Bill. I could only hope that Teddy's family would understand. I made arrangements for flowers. How thankful I was to know that through all the heart ache we had friends lifting us up in prayer, but best of all we had the comfort of knowing that we could turn to God, He is always there to comfort and guide us. He said He would never leave or forsake us. How thankful I am that I turned my life over to Him in 1953. One by one my family in England have left us, with the leaving only Madge and me. Bill's family are all gone except Bob, Kat, and Bill.

The next days were spent bringing Bill home again from hospital and making him comfortable. Sheila was a great help with taking care of her dad, and thought it would solve a lot of running back and forth from one house to the other, if we could sell our houses, and have one built that would be large enough for two families. The three of us talked it over, and decided it would be a good idea. After much planning, figuring, and looking at different houses, we decided to go with the plan. It worked out really well, houses were being built in Grove City, and we checked with one of the builders, and after looked at different plans, we decided on a lot in Grove City.

We went over plans with the builder and chose a house with a full basement that would have two bedrooms, bath, and open spaced lounge, dining area and kitchen plus laundry room. Sheila would have the first and second floor, with first floor entrance hall, half bath, living room, dining room, kitchen, and lounge, and a double-door garage. Upstairs was an on-suite bed and bath, plus three more bedrooms and guest bathroom. All this planning helped Bill take his mind off the thought of having to take chemo.

It took quite some time to finish the house; we enjoyed watching it as each week brought it nearer to completion. We contacted a realtor, and she listed our old house for sale, and because we had done a lot of remodeling it sold quickly. Sheila also had her house listed for sale, and the new house was finally finished and we moved in. Everything was going well and Sheila's old house was quickly sold. She was still grieving over Paul but her time was really filled with having to help move after going work during the day. Bill Jr. Paul, Kathy, and Tom were good to help us; Bill couldn't do very much due to his health.

The house was much larger than both of our old ones, and there was some new furniture to buy. It certainly was a big undertaking to move from two houses. It really is lovely, there is a beautiful lake out back where once was an open field. August 12th Momdane and Bud came up from Kentucky; it was great seeing them again. I missed singing with Mondane. The next day August thirteen Bill had his first chemo treatment at the doctor's office, I was allowed to sit in a chair beside him as he was taking his treatment.

Bill and Michael came over in the evening to cheer him. He was a little dizzy and very restless. I rang the doctor and he prescribed a light sedative to take at bedtime. The next days were spent at the doctor's office, then to the hospital again, Bill was having pain in his side, he had blood tests, and urine tests. His cancer doctor decided the two medicines were too much. Bill ended up with a bowel blockage. The decision was made to discontinue the Vincristine, and just continue an increased dose of the Cytoxin. Mondane and Bud went home, it had been good to have Bud here to help with Bill.

1997 - 1998

Michael had been staying with us for a few days: he was such a pleasant child I loved to entertain him with songs and nursery rhymes, he was very happy to be helping bring his grandpa home from the hospital. August twenty eighth our friend Fritz Baugus, from Grove City Church, came over to visit us. Sunday the thirty first Bill still wasn't able to go to church, I stayed home with him, and in the evening, I took him for a short drive around the community.

September second he was having trouble breathing, another trip to the hospital for tests. I felt so helpless. Sheila and Kathy went to the hospital to be with their dad, and believe it or not, I stayed home and mowed the front lawn. Bill was home again from the hospital feeling a lot better, and was able be out and about while I mowed the remainder of the grass in the back yard. I decided I decided to buy a computer, and because Bill was feeling better, Sheila went with me.

The boys and Kathy have been good to come and spend some time with their dad. I was happy to have a computer and printer. Bill took over the electric typewriter; it gave him something to occupy his time. Saturday September sixth, my birthday, the children all came over to help me celebrate. It was great to see Bill laughing and joking again with the boys. Sunday morning Bill and Sheila went to church for the nine a.m. service. I went to the ten thirty service, and with the help of junior church we assembled and gave out, my Kid Power monthly magazine.

Bill was not feeling well again, I thought maybe it was a little soon to be able to go to church. Tuesday September ninth Bill decided he was able to visit a church member who was having foot surgery. Earl and Frances came to visit; it is great to see Bill feeling some better. The next three months were really tough for him because of the weekly visits to his cancer doctor, series of x-rays, CT scans, and chemo treatments, and many sleepless nights.

There were periods when he was able to attend church, and we spent a lot of time in prayer. Saturday November first, Bill's brother Bob called, and said he would like to come and visit for a while, Paul volunteered to go to Ashland Ky to get Bob, who was eighty seven and not in the best of health, but he was a very jolly person, Paul was very fond of his uncle Bob, and was happy to go and get him. It was a great help having another man in the house, and it gave some relief for Sheila, and me, because Bob was a big help. He stayed until Saturday November fifteenth, when Paul drove him home.

Bill was finally beginning to feel much better. Slowly he began to improve, he was able to attend church regularly, and was able to gradually begin to help Pastor Kevin with visitation and sometimes take charged of Sunday morning services, giving Kevin some time for a short vacation, It was so good to have him so much better. We were able to go to Kentucky to be with Bob. Bill even managed to drive most of the way, when he tired I would take over and drive.

The cancer doctor was very pleased with Bill's progress, the lymph nodes were shrinking, and that was good news. There were still Ct scans, and blood tests, but we felt that he was really getting better, and we were thanking and praising God. November twenty first we had an appointment with the cancer doctor, The CT showed the lymphoma was in remission. It was great to see Bill's day-to-day improvement as he began to regain his strength.

1999

WW received a call from Ashland Kentucky to let us know that Bob was in the hospital, because of him having a light stroke. We consulted with the doctors, and we were told that he would not be able to go home and live by himself. Bill took Bob's keys, and we prepared to stay at his house until we could make plans to take him to our home in Ohio. After more conferences with the doctor, we were informed that we would only be allowed to move him to Ohio after we made preparations to take him to an assisted living establishment. He was held in the hospital until we gave proof of having a place to take him. Sheila, Bill, and I made plans to drive to Ashland to close his house and take care of hospital arrangements.

All was finally completed for Bob to be taken to The Kensington Senior Home, an assisted living place in Columbus Oh, located on Riverside

Drive, a very pleasant area across the road from the river. He was happy for about two weeks, we went to see him every day, and took him for pleasant drives along the banks of the river. He became upset because the some of the residents with Alzheimer's disease who were bothering him at mealtimes, touching his food and he was becoming quite upset about it. I brought it to the attention of the manager, but nothing changed. There was no separation for the well patients, and the Alzheimer patients.

We then transferred Bob to the Sanctuary a lovely place with a private room and a picture window where he could sit and watch for me to arrive every morning between nine and ten o'clock; he was now satisfied. His grandson, Rick came from California and was able to spend some time with him, and as the executor of Bob's estate wanted to make sure all arrangements were made according to Bobs wishes. This eased my mind, because he was not in very good health..

. I received a call at seven a.m. one morning saying Bob had fallen out of bed; but he seemed to be alright; I said I would be there as soon as possible, and as I hung up I awoke Bill to let him know what had happened, and since he wasn't feeling well, I told him I would take care of the situation, and drove the fourteen miles, while all the time worrying about Bob. When I arrived he said he wasn't hurt but was a little shook up. I went to the nurse's station and asked that a rail be attached to the sides of his bed. I continued visiting him every day and I noticed he was becoming a little weaker, and I relied on Sheila to keep an eye on her dad. Sometimes when Bill was feeling better, she would go with me to visit t Bob.

January 2000

January7th was a sad day for me; I received a call from England informing me that Madge had passed away. It was impossible for me to go to her funeral. On the 10th Bill had to go for a C.T. scan; and in the meantime I had received a call from the nurse at the Sanctuary, Bob was not very responsive. After Bill's scan I went to the Sanctuary to check on Bob, he seemed to be doing better. Friday the fourteenth the doctor rang, Bill's Scan was OK, nothing showed up on it. We couldn't understand why he was feeling so bad. Wednesday the nineteenth, Bill still not feeling well, I went to visit Bob and happily to say, he was feeling much better. Friday the twenty first, since Bill was feeling better, Sheila and I went to see Bob.

Saturday and Sunday. I stayed with him all day until late evening, because he was becoming very weak, and I had to feed him a little food, and then went home to get some rest. Early Monday morning I received a call from the Sanctuary, informing me that Bob had fallen out of bed again. I rushed over to the rest home, when I arrived he was barely responding. I phoned Bill to let him know of the situation, he informed me that he and Sheila would be with me shortly. When they arrived we decided that we would all stay with him, because by this time he wasn't responding at all. Hospice came and said it would just be a matter of time before he would be gone.

The Sanctuary provided a room where we could take turns resting, while two of us stayed by Bob's side. There was a time when he was very restless, and we had to ask the nurse for medicine to calm him. At eleven a.m. on Thursday, twenty-seventh of January, he quietly passed away. We called Rick, and he flew into Columbus, Ohio that afternoon. We were relieved when he arrived, and immediately began to take care of funeral arrangements, I turned over to Rick the checking account that Bob had trusted me with, and we all went home to prepare to go to Ashland Kentucky for the funeral. The grandchildren and the few remaining relatives and friends were called. It was a sad time the only ones left now were Kat and Bill. The funeral was held on Monday January 31st.

The next day we packed our bags and said goodbye to relatives and friends, and began the 100-mile journey home to Ohio. Bill was able to drive about half of the way before he tired and I drove the rest of the way. We really missed Bob, and would have no more morning visits to the Rest Home. A short time recently, our son Paul, had made reservations for his family and me to take a trip to England. I didn't think I should go and leave Bill, but Sheila very kindly offered to stay with him and take good care of him. Rebekah, and Andrew, was excited to be able to see the country where their Nana was born.

We left June 14th. This was very exciting for Andrew aged 17 and Rebekah aged 7. We landed in London Heathrow, and finally made it through customs, Paul had stated his wish was to go to London before going to Yorkshire. We were all tired and worn out. As we found transport, and went to our hotel. After a long rest we took a bus ride to see some of London. There was so much to see, Rebekah was thrilled with the underground trains, as we entered, she was fascinated when an attendant quite often loudly called out "Mind the gap." All day long Rebekah went skipping and singing, "Mind the gap." The days past so fast, so much to see and do. Andrew and Rebekah made sure we went to the Theatre one evening. We found our way to Buckingham Palace just in time to see Queen Elizabeth in her open carriage, we were inside the grounds where it was very crowded, and Rebekah was on her daddy's shoulder, we were quite far from the drive way, and it was difficult to see Her Majesty, but from her good seat she yelled, "I can see the Queen, she has a pink hat."

Andrew was taking everything in, and was enjoying everything. We went to Harrods to do some shopping There was so much to see in such an amazingly large, and beautiful, establishment. Rebekah was fascinated with everything; we spent a long time going from floor to floor, trying to see everything, we bought a few items then we were hungry, and tired. Of course I had to suggest we have some of those famous fish and chips. We made quite a few bus rides around the City, the drivers were great at calling out all of the famous places of interest and the homes of famous people. The weather was pleasant and a joy to be sightseeing.

One of the favorite places was the Mews where the horses were kept, one of the horses was so funny he would lower his head when he saw a camera,. Rebekah said she bet he would let her take a picture, we all kidded her and lo and behold, that horse looked up, stuck his head over the gate, and let her take as many pictures as she wished, he also allowed her to stroke his head. After she moved away, that strange horse lowered his head again. We were all sad to leave London, I didn't try to rush them, but I was looking forward to seeing beautiful Yorkshire

We packed our bags and found transport to the nearest car rental, rented a van, and we were on our way, and then came (for me) the scary part, driving on the left side on the road. I was holding my breath, everyone else didn't seem to mind, but I remembered the time I first time I tried to drive on the right side; I was surprised Paul didn't have any trouble with the left side. On the way we stopped to see the stones of the famous Stone-Henge, this was one of Andrews's favorites. We stayed quite a long time Andrew and Rebekah enjoyed the exercise running around each stone. After leaving Stone-Henge we traveled several miles enjoying the lovely scenery when Paul said we should stop for gas.

We stopped at one of the Petrol-Food stops; Paul filled the car with Petrol; Lori stayed with Paul while the children and I went inside the shop to check out the food. Surprise, there was much more than food inside; there was all kinds of candy, all kinds of children's toys, and personal items for travelers. Paul and Lori went inside after filling the tank; Andrew was checking the food; Rebekah was running around checking the toys. She caught sight of her daddy, and ran to him asking if she could have a toy. Lori took control of helping decide what to eat. I can't remember what they chose.

After leaving the shop we all climbed in the van, and were on the road again when the car began shaking and finally stopped. Paul got outside checking to see what the trouble was, and believe it or not he had used Petrol and the van used Diesel. We were on a motor-way (freeway) traffic was heavy but no one would stop, and Rebekah was standing in the grass carrying her doll all the while crying, "I want my Uncle Mark." (He lived in Columbus, Ohio and was a fireman) Poor Lori was trying to calm Rebekah as Paul and Andrew began to walk down the road when in the grass, they saw a sign 'Phone,' Paul picked up the Phone and called for a tow, and after a long wait, a tow truck arrived and we were taken to Scunthorpe, the city where mother had her terribly long hospital stay. The gas tank was emptied and filled with diesel.

After quite a few hours we continued our journey, when Rebekah needed to go to a rest room, we finally found a Rest Area, it was on top of a hill, and Lori had to move things around in the back of the van to tend to Rebekah's needs, when we were ready to leave Lori straightened everything in the back of the van, she then closed the back door. We were driving up the next high hill when the back door of the van came open and our entire luggage went rolling down the hill. We stopped, and Paul and Andrew went running after it. We couldn't help laughing, but Paul wasn't a happy camper.

We were all relieved when nothing else had happened on the way, and we reached York, and were going to find our hotel, when we came to a roundabout with three exits; Paul kept missing his exit and we were all laughing (except Paul) as we kept going around for the third time. He threatened to put us all out of the van if we didn't stop laughing, but before he put us out he found his exit. We finally reached our destination a bed and breakfast at Fulford on the outskirts of York; I was acquainted with the area because that was where my brother Jimmy had lived. The next day after enjoying an English breakfast everyone was anxious to go to York. The manager informed Paul that just across the way was a short road that led to the riverbank side where there was a walkway leading to York.

It was a very short road to the river, and my family couldn't believe how narrow it was. Having been born in Yorkshire it wasn't a bit strange to me, it was just wide enough for one car, and it wasn't a one-Way. There was plenty to see in York, Museum Gardens, the York Minster, which must be seen on the inside, it is awesome; When we were visiting the inside, I asked if any of my four co-travelers would like to climb the 200 steps to the top of York Minster, where beautiful scenery of the town could be seen. No one would take the challenge; even when I told them that during a previous year, when I was visiting, Jimmy and I made it to the top. The street of Shambles is very narrow with no traffic. There was the Viking Village, a great place to see and take a ride around the village.

I don't know much about who the Vikings were because we weren't taught a lot about them in school. I only know that hundreds or thousand years ago the warriors arrived in their giant war ships and landed on the coasts of England, fought, and took over the country. From the little I was told; an occupant of his home was having a basement dug; when a part of a Viking ship was found. it is very interesting to see how an old time village has been assembled from different articles, tools etc., and Viking equipment. I was told that it was one of the favorite places to see. Paul took Andrew and Rebekah out in the evenings to see the shows, which were too tiring for this old gal. I would rather have a comfy chair and a good book to read. One instance I must tell; it was too good not to share.

We had been out sightseeing it was almost dark as we came back by way of the short narrow road. We were almost to the end of the street when Paul said "OH, OH," we all asked what happened, he said, " I broke a Mirror on a parked car, and I don't know which house to go to." After much thinking and worrying, he decided he would wait till the next morning, and then look for a car with a broken mirror and when he found it, he would go to the house where it was parked, apologize, and offer to pay for it. When he arrived back we were all asking questions because he had only been gone such a short time? He told us he didn't find out anything, because every car on that road had broken mirrors.

Kathleen, and her husband Ray, visited us at the B.&.B. I introduced them to Paul, Andrew, and Rebekah. Kathleen said her mother told her she was named after her cousin Kathleen in America. After a very pleasant visit, I told them we were planning to leave the next morning, and said goodbye and promised to keep in touch, they wished us a safe journey home. Time had passed so quickly, and the next morning we packed our bags, making ready for the trip to Manchester Airport.

We said goodbye to everyone at the B&B, where Andrew had made friends with some of the young workers there, and he told them he had enjoyed meeting them, we all said goodbye, and were on our way. We were thankful we had no mishaps on the return journey to the Manchester Airport, where our flight was on time, and after a smooth nine-hour flight were glad to be back in America. I always enjoyed visiting England, but it is always great to be home again.

I was so tired after the long flight and going through customs I don't remember how we got home from the Columbus Ohio Airport, I do remember telling Sheila thanks, for having taken a very good care of her dad while we were gone. September12th I had a right knee replacement I came through it very well, and I was in rehab for a week, and after rehab there was six weeks of therapy, and exercises.

Bill was in much better health, and able each week to take me for therapy, and we ended the year 2000 being able to buy a new car. We hoped and prayed for his health to remain good in the coming year.

CHAPTER

18

2001

So far Bill's health was improving, it was a blessing that his cancer was in recession, and he didn't have to take any more chemo. Sometime later he was having a lot of trouble with his shoulder, and he visited the VA doctor, and was told that it an arrangement would be made to send him to the VA hospital in Dayton Ohio. We were given all necessary instructions for me to take him. If I remember correctly, Sheila and Kathy went with us. It was a long journey but we arrived safely, then there was quite a long time going through procedures before he was settled in a bed.

After he was rested, and it was getting late Sheila and Kathy went with me to find a hotel. We finally found one about 14 miles from the hospital. After I was settled in the hotel, l my girls left for home. The next morning I had some breakfast at the hotel and left early, and when I arrived at the hospital Bill was sleeping soundly A nurse came in to take him for an M.R.I. When we got the results the doctor told him his shoulder wasn't serious but there was some trouble with the Thyroid that needed surgery, and told him what was wrong with it, but I can't remember what it was.

He came through the surgery with no problems, but he had to stay a few days more until he was able to travel. He was happy when he was finally dismissed go home, and so was I. It was a tiresome few days going back and forth from the 14 miles to the hotel in the evening and back to the hospital every morning. He soon made a recovery from the surgery, and his health was improving.

Some great news for Paul Raymond; he had received notice from his Employment; of a promotion to Head Marketer, and supervisor of Market and category management, traveling Coast to Coast. ONLY IN AMERICA THIS IS POSSIBLE OT IS THE AMERICAN DREAM. AND GOD'S BLESSING.

We were proud of our Boys; they worked mighty hard becoming a success. They began early Bill Jr had a successful newspaper route at the age of twelve. They both went half days to High School, and afternoons they began as Bag Boys for Big Bear, and worked hard in the Grocery Business. Bill Jr. stayed with groceries and Paul moved over to deal in marketing. *This was the month when Bill Jr. opened his first GROCERY STORE. Bill SENIOR, Sheila, and I went to the Grand opening,* ONCE AGAIN, THIS COULDN'T HAPPEN IN ANY OTHER COUNTRY THAN AMERICA.

I am telling these facts, not to boast, but to show what is possible, only in America no matter how poor, with hard work, and clean living plus God's help, you can work your way to success that is the American Dream. It is available to anyone. It has taken a long time to reach their dream. We couldn't send them to college, but that didn't stop them. Be happy to be an American, because no other country has the opportunities that are available to you; I love America, *Every good thing that happened to me could only have happened in America.*

2002

Bill was feeling so much better, and Pastor Adkins contacted him; concerning a meeting with regards to the need of an Associate Pastor at Bible Community Church. Bill was thrilled to be able to accept the offer, Pastor Adkins, and Bill, had been friends for several years and worked very well together. I was also offered positions at the church; there was a need for first and second grades at the Christian Academy. Pastor Adkins checked my Qualification, and accepted me as teacher for the two grades.

Because we were both members of the Churches of Christ in Union, (CCCU) we had to secure permission from the Superintendent for a loan to the Bible Community Church, because Bill was recuperating from illness and was presently free from any obligations, we were \ granted the loan with no problems.

I was thankful that I had my certificate from the Children's Evangelistic Association because it qualified me to teach in a Christian

Academy, something I could never have done in England. I also accepted the position of Choir Director for Sunday Morning Services. Bill and I were once again going to be doing what we loved so much. It was such a relief seeing Bill feeling so much better; knowing that every other Sunday Morning he would be in the Pulpit again.

2003

Early in the year we began our Associate Pastorate duties; Jane Brown agreed to be our Choir pianist with practice six p.m. Wednesday evenings before seven p.m. Prayer Meeting. After all these dates and times were agreed upon, and ready to be Okayed by Pastor Adkins, he then gave us a date to begin.

We began our first .Sunday Morning Service with Pastor Adkins opening with prayer. He then introduced Bill as Associate Pastor and mentioned Rev Price was no stranger because he had formerly been Associate a few years ago. The congregation gave him a rousing welcome. Pastor then introduced the Choir, the Director, and the Pianist.

The Service began with Rev Price greeting everyone saying a few words then having the choir to stand and sing, *I'm ashamed to say I can't remember what we sang*. Bill preached a wonderful sermon, and the Service was a success. It was such a pleasure to see him feeling so much better and being back in the pulpit. On weekdays I began teaching first and Second Students at the Christian Academy. It was such a pleasure teaching those small children, they were so excited and worked so hard trying to learn. I began to plan on ways to help with the slow learners.

I was concerned about Wednesdays Chapel for the entire school, because one person was in charge of everyone from Kindergarten to High school classes. I asked for a consultation with Pastor because I attended the chapel and there was a teenage movie being showed, and the younger ones expected to sit still and l pay attention. I asked the young man in charge why there was nothing for the younger children and he replied there was no one to help. I was granted a session with Pastor, and told him my concern for Chapel. He asked if I had any suggestions.

I told him I would like to try taking them in groups of thirty minutes with five minutes allotted to changes of lessons. Beginning with Kindergarten through first, and second grades, then third, fourth and Fifth grades, next Sixth grade and High school girls, and finally Sixth grade and High School boys. That would amount to two hours and twenty minutes to return to class, and next class to enter. Each child must have a readable Bible, and always remember to bring it. I knew it would take a lot of preparing, but it felt that it could manage it. Pastor was happy for me to give it a try.

2004

Began with Bill having a bad fall, thankfully no bones were broken. After several tests, cancer was found on his nose, and on May 10th he began a series of radiation. In the meantime, Paul had purchased tickets for a flight to England, for Lori, Rebekah, himself and me. I told him he would have to cancel my flight because Bill would need me to take him for is radiation treatments. Sheila very generously came to the rescue, since at this time she wasn't working, and she would take her dad to have his radiation treatments. I don't have much recollection of that trip, except as we were on our way down the long steps to the underground I suddenly felt a bit faint; Paul said my face looked gray.

He immediately took me back to the hotel, and .I told him to rejoin his girls, and I would lie down and take it easy, when he finally left to join them. I opened my suitcase to get my Bible, but it wasn't there, I had forgotten to Pack it. I opened the desk drawer, and inside was a Bible, and I removed it and laid it on my chest, and asked the Lord to please help me; I didn't want to have to be taken to the hospital while in England. By the time Paul and the girls came back I was feeling OK, and was able to enjoy the remainder of the trip. If I remember correctly, we went to visit my cousin Kathleen and husband Ray.

I always enjoyed going back to England for a visit, but it isn't my home anymore. I am an American citizen; I love God, and owe a lot to Him for my life, and accomplishments in this beautiful country, and of freedom and opportunities. We arrived home Sheila had taken good care of her dad, and he was in good spirits. The following day, I made an appointment with my doctor and she called the medical center for a Heart Echo Gram. The result was a heart valve problem I can't remember the name for it bit it meant my valve was hardening, I think 40% I was thankful it wasn't any worse.

2005

Bill was feeling much better; Sheila was having lessons regarding grief from losing her husband, Paul Tulloch. She had an appointment on the sixth of March at the Philadelphia Hilton Hotel, for a four day Briefment Facilitator Training Session, in order to be able to personally conduct Grief Support classes. Her wish was to be able to help others deal with grief. It was a nine hundred miles drive, and Bill was concerned about her going alone. Because he was feeling much better, he suggested I should go with her, and if he should need help, he could call Kathy. We finally agreed to take his advice and make sure Kathy was informed, and we were on our way

We left a day early with the intent to travel halfway, arrange to stay overnight in a hotel, and leave early the next morning to arrive at the Hilton in time for the session. It was a pleasant drive, but long and tiring, we enjoyed the scenery, we both enjoyed traveling to new places. We arrived at the Hilton with time to spare. For four days except for mealtimes, I was on my own while Sheila was in training. I went for walks and read books, became bored, and took a nap and sometimes conversed with other guests. Finally the last day of the training was ended, and the next morning we had breakfast and left for home. Sheila was happy with the results of the training and already planning for plans to take it further.

We were enjoying the drive; it was a very cold day, and as we left Philadelphia, horrors, it began to snow. We decided to take the Pennsylvania Turn Pike Toll rd. (*Bad decision*) The further we drove the harder it snowed, the lanes of the Turnpike were very narrow, and the opposite side of the road was busy with semi-trucks, the visibility was bad, but we kept going until we came to an exit for gas. Poor Sheila she couldn't stay on her feet, she tried to step over the gas pump, and fell on her face. A kind gentleman came to her rescue, helped her up, and we were on our way again. I began to wonder if I had been wise in trusting Sheila with our lives.

We finally made the nine hundred miles home in one snowy day by following the salt trucks and praying. Bill was glad to see us; he had made it through the five days without us. June the third, Paul and family moved to a new home in Florida. The same week, Bill was having trouble with his throat; and it was affecting his voice. I made an appointment to see his ENT doctor for a consultation. The doctor wasn't pleased with what he saw, and after certain tests, and a CT. Surgery was scheduled for June third with result of cancer behind his vocal cord. The surgeon talked to us about the result of the surgery, and then after Bill was dismissed from hospital and recovered from surgery, we were to make an appointment for a consultation,

July eighth appointments were made for pre-surgery exams for a second surgery on August third. It was so difficult having consults and tests with doctors, and now we were told; in order to remove all the cancer he will have to one more surgery in six weeks, which took us into September 14th. He'd now had the three surgeries, and I told him I felt so bad for him, his voice was a little better, but not very strong He evidently didn't want to blame God or doctors for his health, I was shocked me when he told me that he had brought all this on himself, the reason being during the war while overseas they couldn't find alcohol, and they drank buzz bomb fluid, combined with his drinking for the seven years after the war. I told him that those had been forgiven in 1953 when he gave his life to God, and all that was in the "Sea of Forgetfulness." I didn't know if he had ever told that to anyone else and I didn't ask him. I just wanted to comfort him.

With all these problems I had arrange to take some time from teaching at the school, but promised the students that I would to be able to take time to help them prepare for the Christmas play that they had been practicing since September. After Bill recuperated from all the surgeries, he wanted to go to Florida. We were both looking forward to seeing the beautiful house that God had blessed him and Lori with. Our head teacher, Miss Linda had promised to help with practice, and Rita took over the choir.

I phoned Paul and Lori and made arrangements to go leave on October 29th; Because Bill didn't want to fly Sheila went with us and drove the 900 miles to Jacksonville Florida; we had enjoyed the journey, and after a very pleasant, enjoyable visit returned home on November seventh returned home November seventh. The Students who had been studying for the Christmas play promised to continue to practice with the help of Miss Linda on Dec. fifteenth.

2006

After all the problems of 2005 I decided to rise early and take a walk when lo, and behold, I fell and skinned my nose on the sidewalk. I was so embarrassed, and got up slowly, looking all around to see if anyone was watching me, thank goodness no one was in sight, what a great beginning of a new day. Bill had risen while I was out walking and falling; His throat was sore from all the radiation treatments, and he was dreading the time when in the days ahead, he was going to be on chemo again. We phoned Paul and Lori and asked if we could go back and stay for a few days to help his dad calm down after all the surgeries. Bill didn't want to fly, and asked Sheila if she would take us in her van, she agreed, and once again we were on our way to Florida.

Paul's house was lovely with plenty of room for all of us, and Sheila planned on returning home the next day. That didn't happen, about two hours after we arrived, Bill went out on the Lanai, where he fell and badly damaged his knee, 911 was called, and the ambulance arrived, and took him to the hospital. Florida was strange to us, and Lori was put to the test helping with all the problems of Ohio insurance, including all the forms and records of his cancer surgeries. It seemed like we were having an awful lot of problems, but God has never let us down. We prayed and asked God for help in these times of these difficult day's sickness, and many of our friends were praying for us.

He was finally admitted in the hospital and ready for knee surgery; after which, the surgeon gave us a report of the condition of the knee; it wasn't good, it was badly injured and would take a long time to heal. On September twenty third he was dismissed from the hospital, and transferred to the Palm Gardens, a facility for rehab, and therapy in Jacksonville, and was to stay there until the doctor was satisfied with the condition of his knee, and would be able to tolerate the journey home to Ohio. Sheila stayed two weeks and was a great help in getting him settled.

It was a very pleasant place; the staff and therapists were very friendly and helpful. I was allowed to visit with him, and attend to his needs every day. For this I was truly thankful, because I could remember my promise never to leave Bill. God always makes a way. Paul's Office was only about five or ten minutes' drive away from the Palms, and he would take me there on his way to work each day, and at six p.m. pick me up on his way home. Usually he would stop in and see his dad; they were long days, and they made the few days I had been with Sheila in Pennsylvania seem like a drop in a bucket.

At first, Bill was a little difficult to please, and was unhappy with having to share a room with another gentleman. I finally arranged to have him changed to a private room. Sheila said she thought he was afraid he would never be able to leave the Palm Gardens. Sometimes he would want me to go to rehab with him; it was difficult watching him go through the therapy, thinking of all he had gone through, the surgeries, chemo, radiation, and now this, I shuddered to see him in so much pain. The staff and therapists were great in dealing with him, trying to help keep his spirit up and encouraging him in every way possible.

The facility was a lovely place with a huge Court Yard with tables and chairs to sit and enjoy the sun, or eat at the tables; every Sunday after attending morning church service Lori would return home to fix a hot dinner, and with the help of Paul and Rebekah a table was set in the court yard for us all to sit and enjoy the delicious food. Bill had to wear a large brace on his knee, and with help of a wheelchair, was able to sit at the table. Sometimes he liked to have me take him out in the courtyard to enjoy the sunshine. He was counting the days until Sheila would arrive and he is well enough to be dismissed. In the meantime, he went every day for therapy, and when he felt like, it an afternoon sitting out in the courtyard soaking up some sunshine'

The time had finally come for a visit from the doctor, to let us know that Bill would be dismissed on October eighteenth, with orders to contact Dr. Gottesman for an appointment, along with forms concerning hospital surgery and therapy he received during his stay at Palm Gardens, because he would need continued therapy for some time. I contacted Sheila, and she came a day early to rest after the long drive, and I was dreading the thought of getting Bill home, it would have been easier on him to fly, but he wanted Sheila to take him in the van.

Plans were made on how to fix a restful place in the back seat, which was no easy task. Finally Paul, and Sheila; with a few helpful hints from onlookers were able make it comfortable as possible. He was carefully helped into the van and we said our goodbyes, and thanks, and were on our way to Ohio.

2007

It was so good to be home again, Bill was doing as well as expected, and I had already made an appointment with Doctor Gottesman for the first day we were back home. I struggled with my memory of this one year, so I only have some notes from Sheila concerning Bill's treatments as follows 'the tumor in his throat was growing, and he began having radiation treatments to be a number of six. I have no idea why I couldn't remember, so to me 2007,and no matter how long I pondered over it the memory was gone, Therefore it will have to stay as is.

2008

Bill received the six radiations that were mentioned previously, and his throat was badly burnt, his voice was raspy, and he could barely speak above a whisper. Early in the year, after the last treatment of radiation, there were more visits with his ENT doctor, and we were told that all that was left was chemo, if and my children had our way there would have been no more chemo, but Bill was alright with the decision, and it was terrible. Week after week I took him for chemo there were other patients in the room all sitting in comfortable chairs, I always stayed in a chair beside him,

One day I was very hungry, and I asked if he would be OK if I left him to get a bite to eat, he told me he would be fine and to go but not to be away long. When I returned he was in a terrible state, because he'd had to go to the rest room, and had to call a nurse to help him, and he said, "don't ever leave me again." I felt awful, because I had never seen him so upset, and I apologized, and promised him I never would leave him again. Sometimes he would be too weak to go for his treatment and I would call to the doctor's, office le t them know and get an appointment for the following week

Late October, his ENT doctor called to check on him, and set up an appointment for a consultation, it was not very pleasant, he stated that the tumor was growing fast, and we both just looked at the doctor and waited to hear the news, and I knew it wouldn't be good. He told us, the tumor was slowly moving and causing Bill to have trouble breathing, and would finally cut off his breathing, I asked the doctor how long he assumed that would be? I looked at Bill, but I couldn't tell how he was feeling, I was holding my breath waiting to hear the next words from the doctor, he looked like he didn't want to tell us, finally he said he was so sorry but it would be about two or three weeks. There are no words to tell how I felt; we thanked the doctor and left holding hands together, and saying nothing. I was trying not to cry.

Something of interest--four of his best friends passed away before him in the in the year of 2008 and he had been in close touch with them, and when they phoned him I had to speak with them for him, and he was too ill to attend any of the funerals, they were as follows, Newell Crawford died June 18, Fritz Baugus died July27 Rev. Ed Adkins died in August, and Rev. Bob Threet, I am not sure of a date and have not been able to contact any of the family, because most of the lived in Pennsylvania.

Bill was too week to stand in the shower and in the meantime I would bathe him the old fashioned way. He thought if I could get him a shower stool maybe he would be able to shower with my help, so I ordered one from the medical store. It was quite a while arriving but on THURSDAY NOVEMBER 20TH I received a call saying the stool was in the store, that same day, I went to Dublin to our Credit Union on business, and Sheila agreed to stay with her dad. On the way home I stopped at the medical store and picked up the stool that he never got to sit in. I realized I had left my p hone at home

I rushed home got out of the car and as I went in the door, Sheila grabbed me and yelled "where have you been, dad can't breathe and he wouldn't let me call the Squad, until you got home call 911." I panicked and asked, "what's the number?" then she panicked, and yelled 9-1-1. I managed to get the call through, and the Squad arrived, and took Bill to the hospital with Sheila and I following and praying. Arriving at the hospital room Emergency we were told he had immediately been taken to the ICU, and suggested we go that area. We found the waiting room in ICU and gave the patient's name also our names, and were told to wait there until Mr. Price was ready to be seen, and then someone take\you to him.

We called all the family in, and the doctor came out and told us he had MRSA in his lungs, which would have come from having an examination on his throat a week before, w sorry to say Bill was dying. We spent three days and nights in the hospital then he was moved to hospital hospice. While was in hospice with family he seemed to linger not able to talk and his breath was getting shorter, and some felt that he was waiting for our 15years old granddaughter Rebekah, who was flying in from Florida to be with him. She finally arrived and leaned over her Papaw loving him and telling how much she loved him and then sang Jesus Loves Me, the song that he so loved to hear her to sing for him, and he closed his eyes listening and he seemed to be more peaceful, and he closed his eyes and died that Tues November twentieth 2:00 a.m.

FUNERAL

COLUMBUS NORTH CHURCH OF CHRIST IN CHRISTIAN UNION

SERVICE   AND EUGULOGY BY REV KEVIN BEHRER

BURIAL AT NORTH GARDENS COLUMBUS, OHIO

He was buried in the Veterans section.

THE EMPTY CHAIR

BY KATHLEEN PRICE

I sit here beside his empty chair

I look, but he's no longer there

God said, it's time for him to go

I never thought I'd miss him so

He's gone to claim that PLACE

To meet JESUS FACE to FACE

He will have his voice once more

And will sing in the Heavenly Choir

After the death of Pastor Adkins the there was no more school or children's church therefore I decided to go to the North CCCU Church with Pastor Kevin, one of my former Junior Church members, he gave me a great welcome, and later I became the Junior Church Director and was happy to be back working for my best Friend, God. I was feeling sad, no Bill, and no Rocky; I had to find a new home for Rocky because he was grieving and he did not like me; we found a very good new owner for him and he was happy again

Sheila had never been to England, and we decided it was time she made the trip. I contacted my cousin Kathleen and we made a list of relatives to get in touch with, and she agreed to phone them and invite as many as possible to join us for a get acquainted dinner party for Sheila. It took quite a lot of time since we would like to find a place that did dinner and had a courtyard; Kath finally found the old Lodge located at Malton N. Yorkshire.

Finally it was settled and we set a date. Sept 23 Sheila and I made our plans for a flight to Manchester and a Bed and breakfast, also transport from the airport to our destination since there was no Jimmy or Teddy to call on. We finally made it to York and the B& B, settled in. It wasn't the greatest but it was clean with two small rooms and the breakfasts were good. The next day my cousin Margaret (*Kathleen's sister0* and husband were kind and arrived at the B&B to take us to the Lodge. If I remember correct there were 35 in attendance. Kath had everything arranged and we had a lovely time meeting relatives.

We had an enjoyable time, Mandy took us to a Castle one day, the only trouble was it rained so hard it was too wet and muddy to get to the Castle but there was a lovely cafe and gift shop on the grounds, one thing is sure about England you can always count on the rain. We were a bit bound by not being able to drive, but there was plenty to see in York but our legs would only take us so far. We had a great time and began to talk about a next trip with better lodgings. Finally it was time for our transport to Manchester and long flight home.

BAD NEWS

My oldest son Bill had an accident at one of his stores. He fell off the dock while lifting something heavy to put in trash. He crushed his arm and he was in the hospital in Dayton, Sheila and I rushed to the hospital. He had already been in surgery and he had a bionic arm when they finished with him. I was so thankful he was alive. Later after he was able to be home Rhonda had a hospital bed in the front room and I packed up what I needed and went to stay and help Rhonda until he was able to take care of himself.

Rhonda took great care of him and I was able to take care of his bed and other household needs. He continues to have a lot of problems with his back and foot but God has been good to him.

THE END OF A MINISTRY

On my ninetieth birthday my children gave me a surprise birthday Party at the North Church and made me Queen for a day, it was a lovely surprise and many of my former Junior Church Children, now adults, were there. A lovely dinner was served. It was a day to always remember. My girls had made a large board of pictures of lots of memories of the past. It was a big day for me, I resigned from my position of Junior Church, and it was time to hand it over to younger workers. I did have one last accomplishment before leaving,

It was at our Kid Power for Missions yearly service to turn in money we collected that year. I first set a goal of one thousand dollars at the beginning of the year. As the time passed the children were really working hard each month and I changed the goal to two thousand dollars. Pastor Kevin thought that might be too much, but that made the children more determined. With lots of help from the adults, and when the night of the service came to hand in our amount, we had made our two thousand and a few dollars more. What a great cheer went up for the North Church winner and so with that good feeling I retired. Thus ended my sixty-seven years of working for my LORD AND THE COUNTRY that I love so well,

At the time I am writing this I recently had my ninety- fourth birthday. Sheila and I were blessed to make 3 trips to England after Bill's passing.

We had one more trip in 2014. Paul took Sheila and me first class to England. This was our first time flying first class and the new Pod sleeper had just been put in .I almost felt like a Queen and what service we got all night long.

My two Boys "THE PRICE BROTHERS " with hard work and God's help and blessing and this great country of ours that no other country can do have made the American dream.

I have been active, until the Covid 19 Pandemic, at the Evans Senior Center. I participated in their actor's group, putting on comedy plays for the local community and was on the WII Bowling League.

How good God has been to this poor, one time Yorkshire girl. I love this country, God's Country. It has been 74 years since I stepped on American soil and time goes on until the Lord says its tine to go.

This is Dedicated to God and My Country-America

The House Where I Was Born

My Mother

Granny And Granddad Lincoln

My Stepdad And Mother With Jiminy

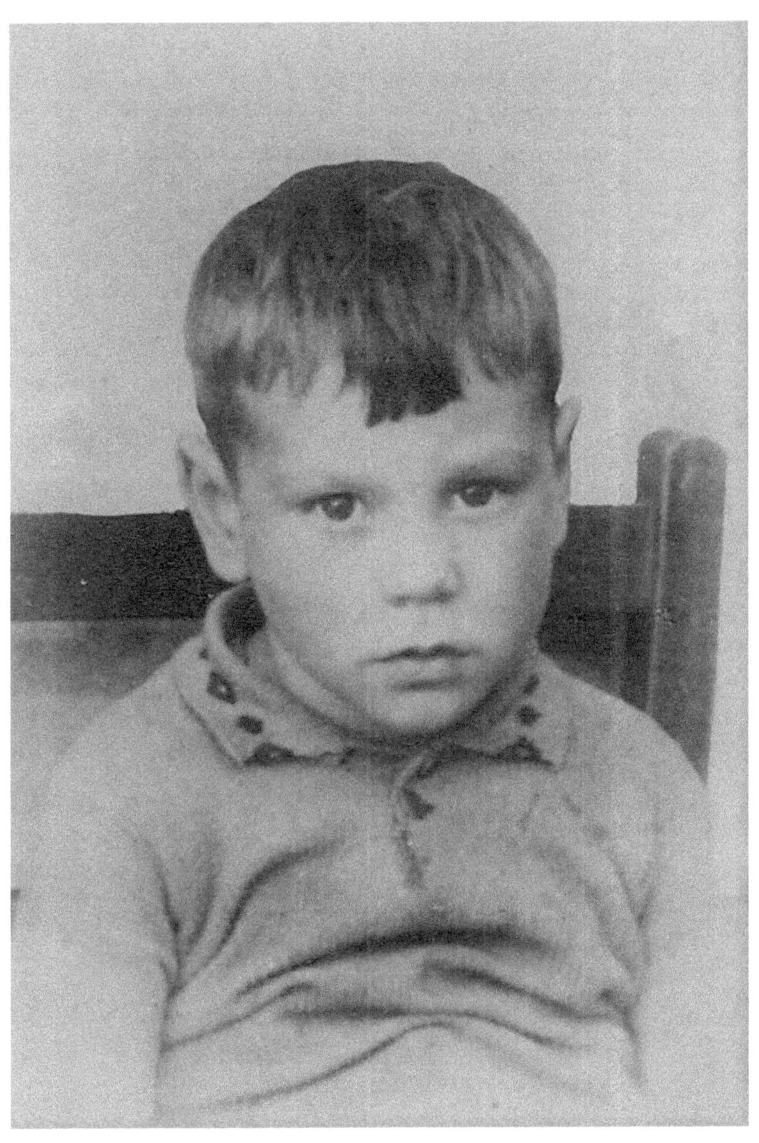

My Brother Raymond (Poggy)

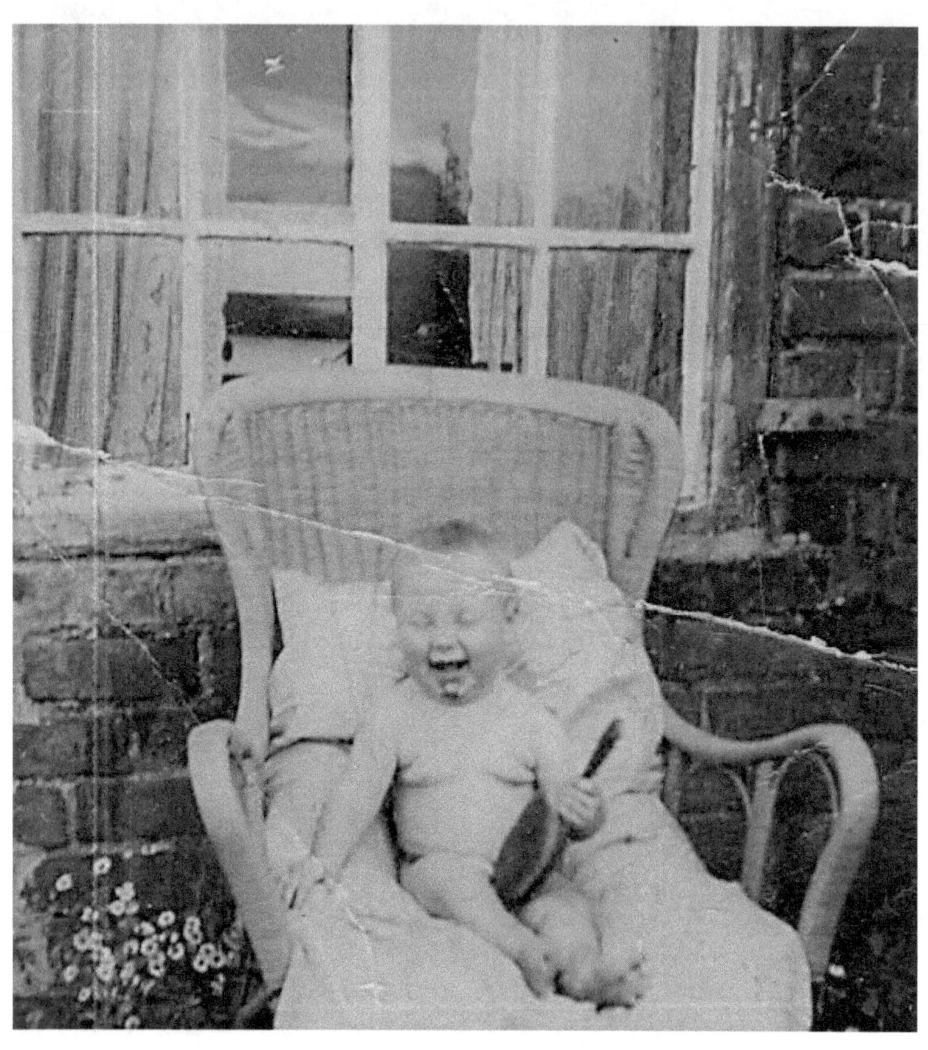

My brother Michael

Me and Poggy with Jimmy in the back

Jimmy on the farm

Bill with his Army-Air Force uniform-1943

Bill with his Army-Air Force uniform

Billy and I dating in 1944

<table>
<tr><td colspan="2">ASF - NEW YORK PORT OF EMBARKATION
PORT TRANSPORTATION DIVISION
58TH STREET & 1ST AVENUE
BROOKLYN, NEW YORK
ITINERARY SHEET</td><td colspan="2">SCHEDULE PREPARED FOR

KATHLEEN PRICE   19 -57</td><td>DATE PREPARED

1946</td></tr>
<tr><td colspan="2">ITINERARY</td><td>RAILROAD</td><td>TIME</td><td>DATE</td></tr>
<tr><td>LV.</td><td>NEW YORK</td><td>NYC 11</td><td>7;30P</td><td>5/27/46</td></tr>
<tr><td>AR.</td><td>COLUMBUS, OHIO</td><td></td><td>11;10 A</td><td>5/28/46</td></tr>
<tr><td>LV.</td><td></td><td>C&O 46</td><td>10;50 P</td><td>"</td></tr>
<tr><td>AR.</td><td>ASHLAND KY</td><td></td><td>1;15 A</td><td>5/29/46</td></tr>
<tr><td>LV.</td><td></td><td></td><td></td><td></td></tr>
<tr><td>AR.</td><td></td><td></td><td></td><td></td></tr>
<tr><td>LV.</td><td></td><td>SS TYLER</td><td></td><td></td></tr>
<tr><td>AR.</td><td></td><td></td><td></td><td></td></tr>
<tr><td>LV.</td><td></td><td></td><td></td><td></td></tr>
<tr><td>AR.</td><td></td><td></td><td></td><td></td></tr>
<tr><td>LV.</td><td></td><td></td><td></td><td></td></tr>
<tr><td>AR.</td><td></td><td></td><td></td><td></td></tr>
<tr><td>LV.</td><td></td><td></td><td></td><td></td></tr>
<tr><td>AR.</td><td></td><td></td><td></td><td></td></tr>
<tr><td>LV.</td><td></td><td></td><td></td><td></td></tr>
<tr><td>AR.</td><td></td><td></td><td></td><td></td></tr>
<tr><td>LV.</td><td></td><td></td><td></td><td></td></tr>
<tr><td>AR.</td><td></td><td></td><td></td><td></td></tr>
<tr><td>LV.</td><td></td><td></td><td></td><td></td></tr>
<tr><td>AR.</td><td></td><td></td><td></td><td></td></tr>
</table>

INSTRUCTIONS — 1. If you, or any of your children should become sick on the train, inform the Train Conductor or the Train Commander. 2. If any difficulty is encountered at transfer points, consult the Travelers Aid Bureau, the Red Cross, or the Military Police. RAILROAD SCHEDULES ARE SUBJECT TO CHANGE WITHOUT NOTICE

TC-2 FORM
REV 15 MAR 1946 1084

Itinerary Street for trip to Ashland

My wedding

Bill And I With Our Newborn-Sheila

Living in the Pines-Ashland, Kentucky

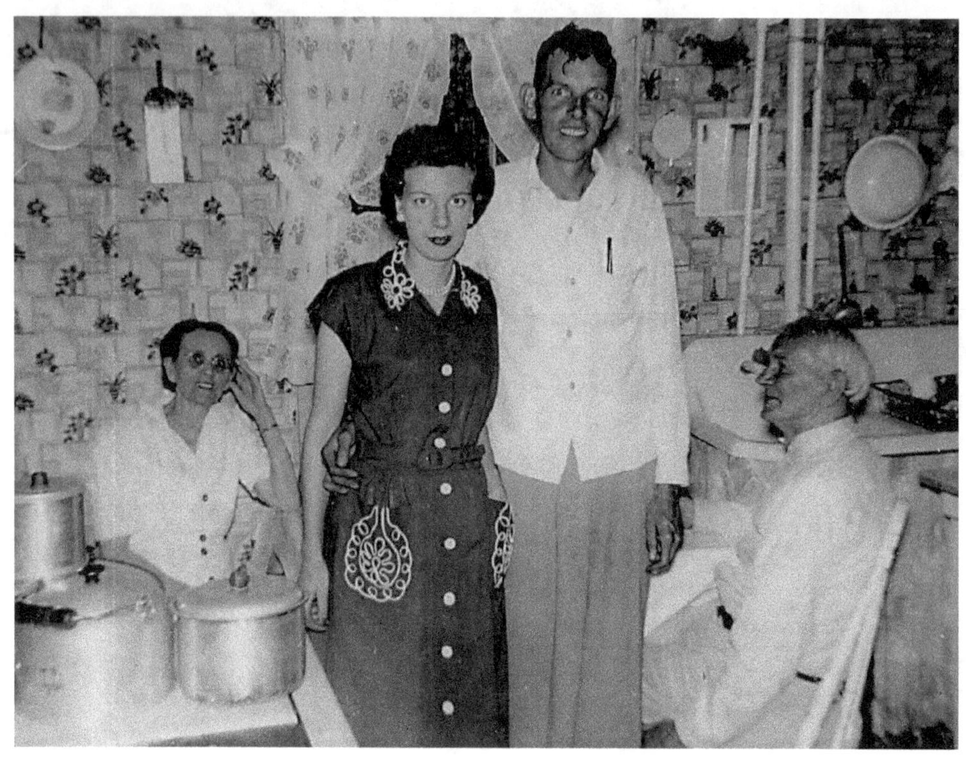

Bill And I At Mom And Dad's

My Mother, Father And Mother-In-Law Price And Sheila

Our Young Family In 1960

Bill And I, Bills Mother,
And Our Four Children; Sheila, Kathy, Bill And Paul.

Our First Church In Cannonsburg, Kentucky

Citizenship Certificate

REV. BILL PRICE

Brother Price is the Co-Evangelist for the Rescue Hour. God also is using him as the printer of the "Rescue Hour Herald".

His spirit-filled preaching has been a blessing to many as he has conducted Revivals in the Tri-State area. Also as a radio preacher he has reached hundreds with the full gospel of Christ.

Brother Price is open for Revivals in the future. He can be contacted through the Rescue Hour mailing address: Elwood Gibbs, Box 632, Ashland, Kentucky.

Bill Working With The Rescue Mission

THE RESCUE HOUR TRIO

These are spirit-filled Christians who sing on the
T. V. and radio programs.
From left to right: Dorla Gamble, the sister of Bro.
Gibbs; Kathleen Price, the wife of Bill Price; Mon-
dane Horne, the pianist.
Sister Price is originally from England and was con-
verted after her arrival in America.

Here I Am With The Rescue Hour Trio

My Brother Jim And Me

My Brother Ted In 1951 Before I Found Him

My First School

The Six Bells In England Where I First Met Bill

On My 90th Birthday In Front Of Class
That I Taught In Junior Church When They Were Children.

Me At Evans Senior Center During A Comedy Presentation